MW00532394

Praise for

If you want to rise up and make...
and your community, read this book. To be victorious, which God wants
for you, you must appropriate God's strengths and weapons. I benefited
from so many of Judy's explanations, stories, and challenges, and you will,
too. I needed her insights and refreshing, vulnerable, and accurate explanations of relevant Scripture. Passages came alive! And her prayers! They'll
mature me and give me hope. I'll be reading them often. Truths here will
allow you to become who you know you want to be—an equipped and
powerful warrior in God's army!

KATHY KOCH, founder of Celebrate Kids, Inc., and author of *Five to
Thrive, 8 Great Smarts*, and other titles

If you long for courageous faith, authentic truth, righteous living, and a prayer
life that faces fear and uncertainty head-on, look no further. In *The Loudest
Roar* author Judy Dunagan teaches us to defeat the enemy and stand firm in
the mighty strength of our powerful Lion of Judah! This book gave me tools
to develop my "roar" in the face of disappointment, discouragement, temptation, and unfulfilled expectations. Read this treasure on your own, or better
yet, with a group of friends who will explore the "Going Deeper" section
together. The prayers in the back of the book give you everything needed to
roar like our Lion, and to send the enemy whimpering away.

CAROL KENT, Executive Director of Speak Up Ministries, speaker,
and author, *When I Lay My Isaac Down*

This book on spiritual warfare is optimistic, realistic, and personally applicable. I appreciated Judy's candor in sharing her personal struggles and
even those within her own marriage. This is a book that can be given to
any Christian, knowing that all of us need to be reminded that we are in
a winnable battle with our unseen enemy, whose roar is drowned out by
the louder roar of the Lion of the Tribe of Judah. The book is a wonderful
reminder that we are serving a King who has already won!

ERWIN W. LUTZER, Pastor Emeritus, The Moody Church, Chicago

We all face times in our lives when the enemy feels more real than God. At such times, we need encouragement and guidance on how to pray with wisdom and live with faith. In *The Loudest Roar*, Judy Dunagan weaves together profound insights from Scripture with clear guidance gleaned from years of experience that you will find both helpful and encouraging. There are too few good books on our victory in Christ and warfare praying, and Judy has written a masterpiece you will want to read again and again.

MARCUS WARNER, President of Deeper Walk International

If we are honest, we often live from a place of defeat. We buckle under the roar of the enemy, his accusations, his lies, his temptations. We can feel powerless. In *The Loudest Roar*, with personal stories and practical biblical wisdom, Judy Dunagan brilliantly teaches us how to hold our thoughts captive to Christ, stand firm in our faith, and truly live from a place of victory in Jesus. This beautiful book will equip you for the battle, remind you that God is near, and that the Lion of Judah is your protector and defender. You will be reminded you are not alone in the battle as you train your ears and heart to trust in the loudest roar.

LISA BISHOP, Director of Women's Ministry, Park Community Church, life coach and founder of Living a Life Unleashed, LLC

We live in a world where the enemy's lies bombard us around every corner, taunting us to be crippled in fear, helplessness, and hopelessness. For that reason, I'm so grateful for Judy Dunagan's powerful and practical encouragement in *The Loudest Roar*. It will awaken a fight within your spirit to the truth and confidence that we serve the Lion of Judah, whose strength and presence empower us to battle sin, fight our fears, and live boldly in the battle that He has already won. Let these words wash over you with fresh hope and strength for whatever you're facing.

SARAH WALTON, author of *Tears and Tossings, Hope When It Hurts,* and *Together Through the Storms*

For the moments in the journey when you dare to admit that it seems God may be unaware or worse, unconcerned about what you're going through, *The Loudest Roar* is a spirit-renewing gift. Judy invites you and me to pray for restoration of wonder, in brave acceptance of the fact that even though God's ways are not our ways, we are never forsaken or forgotten. And no matter what you see with your eyes and feel in your soul, He is in fact orchestrating a symphony of grace so that your song of faith will echo throughout and inspire generations to come for good. *The Loudest Roar* is an invitation to discover that even when your story is shattered, He is faithful, true, and ever worthy of praise.

JUNI FELIX, author, radio host, speaker, and member of Dr. BJ Fogg's Stanford Behavior Design Teaching Team

Anxiety. Fear. These are the diseases of our age. The words "Courage, Dear Heart," which begin this book, breathe hope into weary and troubled hearts. I first knew Judy as a missionary on our staff in Vienna. I've watched this hope-filled message grow in her for over thirty-five years. True teaching plus practical "how to" fill these pages. You need this book! I highly recommend it!

LINDA DILLOW, missionary and author, *Calm My Anxious Heart* and *Satisfy My Thirsty Soul*

The Loudest Roar is a much-needed book for today, filled with truth and wisdom. Judy writes with clarity, strength, and warmth, inviting the reader to take hold of everything that Christ has taken hold of for us. Reading it will empower you to understand your position of authority in Christ and how to live in the victory that Jesus has won for us. Read it. Underline it. Marinate in it. Take it to heart. Make it your own.

STASI ELDREDGE, *New York Times* bestselling author, *Captivating*

You will be blessed as you read this book authored by a very special servant of God. Her father was used by God to help many believers discover their freedom and authority in Christ, and now his gifted daughter continues this legacy in equipping the church with this book! The prayer of Scripture is for each believer to know in their experience hope that overcomes despair, their inheritance that dislodges lies, and the power that raised Jesus from the dead and seated Him in His place of authority (Eph. 1:18–21). May this book be used by God to enable many to personally discover the answer to this prayer.

BILL THRASHER, author and professor, Moody Theological Seminary

Almost ten years of prayer ministry experience has taught me that most believers feel defeated or inept in the area of prayer. As the enemy roars loudly, we simply cannot afford to be a prayerless person, let alone a prayerless generation. *The Loudest Roar* is a clarion call and victory cry that will offer hope to the quaking heart, a road map to those wondering how to begin, and equipping to those already warring on their knees. Judy Dunagan is a kind and relatable companion on this journey. You're going to love her. But even more, don't be surprised if you close this book, fist pump the victory that is yours, and get on your knees. Hallelujah, victory is sure.

LEE NIENHUIS, author, speaker, prayer warrior, and original host of the *Moms in Prayer Podcast* for Moms in Prayer International

In this powerful book, Judy combines an abundance of Scripture with moving personal stories to declare the truth about the supremacy of Christ, and the strength and power we possess for spiritual battles we face. I was comforted again and again by the reminders of our Lord's intimate and constant companionship that assures us we have nothing to fear. I predict you will return often to this book when you are in battles that threaten to overwhelm you. I invite you to open your heart to hear God's truth and be led deeply into worship as you read this wonderful book.

PAMELA MACRAE, professor, Moody Bible Institute, Ministry to Women and Ministry to Victims of Sexual Exploitation

LIVING IN THE UNSHAKABLE
VICTORY OF CHRIST

THE
LOUDEST ROAR

JUDY DUNAGAN

MOODY PUBLISHERS
CHICAGO

Edited by Amanda Cleary Eastep
Interior design: Brandi Davis
Cover design: Erik M. Peterson
Cover illustration of lion copyright © 2019 by bankapollo / iStock Photos (1132032138). All rights reserved.
Author photo: Kelly Callewaert

Library of Congress Cataloging-in-Publication Data

Names: Dunagan, Judy, author.
Title: The loudest roar : living in the unshakable victory of Christ / Judy Dunagan.
Description: Chicago, Il : Moody Publishers, [2022] | Includes bibliographical references. | Summary: "Do you feel stuck in the same battles? With this book, you'll marvel at the power, majesty, and authority of Jesus and learn how to stand in His unshakable victory. God's roar over you becomes your roar, diminishing the lies of the enemy . . . to a whisper"-- Provided by publisher.
Identifiers: LCCN 2022014731 (print) | LCCN 2022014732 (ebook) | ISBN 9780802427960 | ISBN 9780802476333 (ebook)
Subjects: LCSH: Christian life. | Success--Religious aspects--Christianity. | BISAC: RELIGION / Christian Living / Prayer | RELIGION / Christian Living / Inspirational
Classification: LCC BV4509.5 .D86 2022 (print) | LCC BV4509.5 (ebook) | DDC 248.4--dc23/eng/20220413
LC record available at https://lccn.loc.gov/2022014731
LC ebook record available at https://lccn.loc.gov/2022014732

Originally delivered by fleets of horse-drawn wagons, the affordable paperbacks from D. L. Moody's publishing house resourced the church and served everyday people. Now, after more than 125 years of publishing and ministry, Moody Publishers' mission remains the same—even if our delivery systems have changed a bit. For more information on other books (and resources) created from a biblical perspective, go to www.moodypublishers.com or write to:

Moody Publishers
820 N. LaSalle Boulevard
Chicago, IL 60610

1 3 5 7 9 10 8 6 4 2

Printed in the United States of America

In loving memory of my father
Mark I. Bubeck

who taught me the truths in this book
from the time I was a little girl

and

Dedicated to my beloved husband
Rick Dunagan

who has bravely fought the good fight to live
out these truths with me
for our children and grandchildren

and

In honor of King Jesus,
the Lion of Judah

"He only is my rock and my salvation,
my fortress; I shall not be shaken."
Psalm 62:6

CONTENTS

INTRODUCTION

MADDIE'S STORY WAS one of the hardest stories I have ever heard, even though I'd been in women's ministry leadership at our church for many years. She asked to meet with me for some biblical counseling and encouragement. She was facing battles in many areas of her life, including watching her child walk away from his faith and her husband walk away from their marriage. She was on the brink of despair and questioning God's goodness and faithfulness.

We spent quite a bit of time together as I listened and prayed with her. But after we said goodbye, I felt somewhat defeated, as if the enemy had more power over this woman's life than God did. Closing the door to my office, I cried out to Him, praying, *Your Word tells us that the enemy prowls around like a roaring lion, seeking someone to devour.*[1] *Why does he have so much power?*

Immediately I sensed the Lord whispering to my heart, "Yes, Judy, but I am the Bigger Lion with the Louder Roar! I am the Lion of Judah, and I am on the throne!"

Now, I'm not putting words into God's mouth. His Word shows us from Genesis through Revelation that we have a powerful enemy intent on our destruction.[2] But, though the roar of the enemy of our soul can seem deafening, the truth is that our Almighty God—the rescuer of our souls—is the *bigger lion with the loudest roar.*

The Bible refers to our Lord Jesus Christ as the Lion of the tribe of Judah in a glorious scene in heaven that the apostle John paints for us in Revelation 5. In verse 2 an angel cries out, "Who is worthy to open the scroll and break its seals?" The answer comes in verse 5: "Weep no more; behold, the Lion of the tribe of Judah, the Root of David, has conquered."

Read these words out loud: "The Lion of the tribe of Judah, the Root of David . . . has conquered!" Our King of kings has conquered death and despair, sin and Satan! And the victory Jesus has won for us should be the loudest "roar" over us.

But do we live like a people whose King has conquered? Or do we let the roars of this world, our sin, and Satan drown out the truth of God's Word and His mighty power that promise us victory in Jesus?

As we journey through this book together, we will learn how to faithfully pick up our mighty weapons of God's Word, His armor, and prayer in order to stand firm and daily live in the victory that Jesus has already won for us.

- We will first turn our eyes toward the "Bigger Lion"—our Lord Jesus Christ—and see how His power, majesty, and authority are what gives us courage and assures our promised victory.
- Then, in Part Two, we will learn how to apply those truths to our everyday lives in practical ways. We'll see that Jesus is our armor and how we can live in His unshakable victory when we choose faith over fear, victory over sin, and truth over lies.
- We will look at how to wear our armor—as outlined in Ephesians 6:10–18—boldly, proudly, and securely because

of who Jesus is. We will see how He covers us with *His* armor of salvation (helmet), *His* righteousness (breast-plate), *His* truth (belt), *His* peace (shoes), *His* faithfulness (shield), and *His* living Word (sword of the Spirit).

- In Part Three, "Our Mightiest Roars," we'll discover ways to daily pick up the sword of the Spirit—God's Word—as our weapon against the different enemies we have coming at us.
- And, we will end the book looking at how the Roar of Prayer is also a mighty weapon and the key to dwelling in our protective covering of His armor. You'll find practical and creative ways to awaken a fresh commitment to prayer and how to pray Scripture over loved ones.

At the end of most chapters, you will find a written prayer that you can pray aloud or use as a prompt to journal your own prayers. I've also suggested worship songs to listen to—related to the truths in the book—and I've created a "Loudest Roar Worship" playlist with those same songs that you can access at my website, judydunagan.com.

As a bonus, in the back of the book you'll find practical ways to go deeper with the content—either on your own or in a small group, book club, or Bible study setting. This Going Deeper section includes questions and journaling prompts to help you apply the truths in the book to your own life.

My hope behind this book is that instead of living in defeat, we will become battle-ready and know how to fight for truth to prevail over our own hearts and minds, as well as over those we love.

Imagine if the loudest voice over you is the roar of the victory that Jesus has already won for you.

Imagine if that inner voice that often whispers in your heart and mind, making you feel defeated, could immediately be discerned and silenced by truth.

Imagine that when you worry about the safety or future for your family, instead of being overcome with fear, you can dwell in peace no matter your circumstances.

Imagine how it will feel the next time you're tempted but you turn to Him as your rescuer from sin.

Imagine if the doubts or lies you have been believing about God, or about who you are in Christ, are silenced with truth.

Imagine if you can move from longing to be a prayer warrior to actually becoming one.

My prayer is that once you've read through this book you will be more equipped and empowered to believe and live in God's unshakable victory—diminishing the enemy's roar to a whimper.

part one

THE
BIGGER
LION

I love you, O Lord, my strength.
The Lord is my rock and my fortress and my deliverer,
my God, my rock, in whom I take refuge,
my shield, and the horn of my salvation, my stronghold.
I call upon the Lord, who is worthy to be praised,
and I am saved from my enemies.

PSALM 18:1–3
A PSALM OF DAVID, THE SERVANT OF THE LORD

chapter one

COURAGE, DEAR HEART

"Have I not commanded you? Be strong and courageous.
Do not be frightened, and do not be dismayed,
for the LORD your God is with you wherever you go."

JOSHUA 1:9

WE STOPPED DEAD IN OUR TRACKS as the lion began to roar. My toddler grandson was just a few steps ahead of us, closest to the huge animal. The majestic lion, with his gorgeous, black-tipped mane, towered above Liam, who had his nose pressed against the wall of protective glass. Liam was enamored by the animal's mighty roar echoing throughout the zoo that sat tucked up against a mountain in Colorado Springs.

Liam stood tall and brave, as he tapped on the safety glass with a challenging, "Hey, you!" as if to say, "Be quiet, you don't scare me!" The video we took of the brave little boy scolding the roaring lion will remain a family favorite.

Male lions use their mighty roar to "scare off intruders, warn the pride of potential danger and show off power among other males." The second largest in the cat family, it's the lion that has the loudest roar that can be heard from as much as five miles away.[1]

The lion's roar over Liam may not have been heard five miles away, but it was loud enough to make us stand in awe and wonder of that magnificent creature, and grateful for the protective glass between us.

The decibel of a lion's roar is relevant to what I believe God wants each of us to know about our victory and position in Christ and what we will be studying throughout this book together.

In the introduction, we looked at how Jesus is called the Lion of the tribe of Judah in Revelation 5. I assume that the depiction of Him as a lion is part of the reason author C. S. Lewis chose to make the Christ figure in *The Lion, the Witch and the Wardrobe* a lion named Aslan. Most likely you've read that classic book or watched the movie adaptations. In an oft-quoted exchange between young Lucy and the Beavers when they first tell her about Aslan, Lucy expresses her fear of meeting a lion. The Beavers address the girl's fear by telling her that although Aslan isn't safe, he's good and he's the king.

Lucy is my favorite of the four siblings in the Chronicles of Narnia. Though the youngest, she seems the bravest and the one closest to Aslan, ever-aware of him and his love, protection, and sacrifice for them. Later in the series we find Lucy surrounded by danger in *The Voyage of the Dawn Treader*. At one point she hears a voice that "whispered to her, 'Courage, dear heart,' and the voice, she felt sure, was Aslan's."[2]

May the truths in this book whisper (or roar) "Courage, dear heart" over you as you walk this groaning earth and face battles with fear, temptation, lies, and even doubts about God's goodness, protection, and faithfulness.

OUR ENEMY

God's Word tells us that we have an enemy intent on our destruction. He is likened to a lion that is far from good and definitely not safe.

First Peter 5:8 tells us: "Your adversary the devil prowls around like a roaring lion, seeking someone to devour."

My father, Mark Bubeck, teaches about Christ's victory over the enemy's roars in his books *The Adversary* and *Warfare Praying: Biblical Strategies for Overcoming the Adversary*. One of my favorite quotes from *Warfare Praying* is:

> Satan roars to make us afraid and thus more vulnerable, but our purchased right is courage to resist him.[3]

Sadly, instead of courage, we often choose to live in fear and defeat, with little understanding of how to stand in the courage and victory Christ has already purchased for us through His death, resurrection, and ascension. We can get overwhelmed by the enemy's roars to the point that we no longer hear the loudest roar of our mighty God and the truth of His Word. We can easily forget that God is our refuge, our mighty fortress, our strong deliverer.

Recently, I've heard some followers of Christ—even those who have known Him for decades—talk about how it seems that Satan's power is increasing and he is winning. Many are living in defeat, as if the roar of the enemy is louder than the roar of the Lion of Judah. They seem to be forgetting all that Jesus has won for us.

There are others who haven't thought much about the enemy's roars or haven't discerned his attacks on their lives. Some Christ followers choose to ignore the importance of understanding more about our position of victory over the enemy because they think if they ignore him, he'll leave them alone.

Then there are others who doubt that

We can get overwhelmed by the enemy's roars to the point that we no longer hear the loudest roar of our mighty God and the truth of His Word.

the enemy even exists and view him as a silly fictional character in horror movies. That can be dangerous thinking. God's Word teaches us that the enemy is a formidable foe and that we need to know how to boldly stand against him. He wants to lull us into complacency or ignorance about his schemes and tactics and to not take him seriously.

I wonder if the apostle Paul had similar concerns for believers when writing to the church in Ephesus, a city steeped in worship of false gods. Paul wrote this victory cry for the Ephesians even while he was imprisoned in Rome for his teachings and his faith in Christ:

> Finally, be strong in the Lord and in the strength of his might. Put on the whole armor of God, that you may be able to stand against the schemes of the devil. For we do not wrestle against flesh and blood, but against the rulers, against the authorities, against the cosmic powers over this present darkness, against the spiritual forces of evil in the heavenly places. Therefore take up the whole armor of God, that you may be able to withstand in the evil day, and having done all, to stand firm. (Ephesians 6:10–13)

Though those words were written thousands of years ago, that victory cry is also for us today. As followers of Christ, we battle the enemy, our own sin, and this clamoring-for-our-attention world that can threaten to overtake us with fear, distraction, temptation, resentment, and even doubt about the power, protection, and nearness of our God. But our Most High, Almighty God is the Victor. He is the Lion of Judah with the loudest roar. And because of Him, we can "be strong *in* the Lord and in the strength of *his* might." While we are not alone in our battles because God is with us, we do need to know how to "stand against the schemes of the devil" . . . and "take up the whole armor of God, that (we) may be able to withstand in the evil day, and having done all, to stand firm."

My father began writing his first book, *The Adversary,* in the early seventies, right around the time when it seemed our culture was becoming more enamored with fortune-telling, séances, and other occult practices. He was a young pastor at that time and a prayer warrior with a deep burden for revival to sweep across our globe. He would often pray early in the morning, crying out for revival in his own life, his family's, his congregation's, and the world. At that time, the Holy Spirit impressed on his heart that he needed a better understanding of how to battle the enemy who would try to thwart revived lives at all cost.

My father diligently searched the Scriptures to learn more about our victory in Christ. He studied passages like Ephesians 6, 1 Peter 5, and Psalm 91. He connected with other pastors and seminary professors who could teach him more about our protection and how to stand firm against the enemy's tactics to try to defeat us.

I was only twelve years old when Dad was researching for his first book, and he often taught me about the truths he was studying. I was struggling with some debilitating fears and nightmares at that time. I had naively dabbled with séances and Ouija boards at slumber parties when I was in middle school, which to this day saddens my heart, knowing God's Word carefully warns us about the danger of such things.[4]

But my dad was like a lion protecting his cub, often praying for me as the enemy tried to prey over me with fear as I tried to fall asleep. I remember Dad kneeling by my bedside and often praying God's Word over me. Through that, he taught me about God's covering of His armor as outlined in Ephesians 6. He encouraged me to memorize the pieces of the armor,[5] and I learned to pray the victory roar of God's Word from Ephesians 6:10–18 and Psalm 91, and many other Scriptures. I continue to pray through those passages today over my own family, decades after I began to find my roar against the enemy as a seventh grader.

In recalling my dad teaching me those truths, I couldn't help but think of a poignant scene in the movie *The Lion King*. The tiny lion cub Simba is facing the vicious cackle of hyenas intent on tearing him to pieces. Young Simba is trying to squeak out a roar to scare them away, but the hyenas just mock his attempts. Suddenly, Simba appears to let out a mighty roar beyond his ability, and shocked, the hyenas retreat in fear. For a few seconds, young Simba thinks it's because of his own brave roar that they back off; but the reason they've retreated is because Simba's father—a strong warrior lion—has stepped up behind him and displayed his mighty roar against Simba's enemies.

That is what our mighty God does for us. It's His mighty roar of victory covering us that becomes *our* roar and makes the enemy flee in defeat. (We are going to discover more about what our roar looks like in future chapters.)

Today we might feel like little Simba with no real voice of victory against our enemy; or it can seem as if the enemy's roar is getting louder on many fronts. He wants us to think that, and to give up in defeat or complacency. Instead, may we truly know we can "be strong in the Lord and in the strength of his might" (Ephesians 6:10). We are going to dive deeper into those verses in Ephesians 6 and the armor in Part Two of this book. But before that, let's turn our eyes upon Jesus and all that He has won for us as our protector.

JESUS IS OUR PROTECTIVE BARRIER

Just like little Liam had the courage to stand up against a roaring lion because of the protective barrier between them, we too have all that we need to fight the mighty roars of the enemy of our souls because Jesus provides our protective barrier.

Let me say that again another way—it is only because of Jesus Christ that we can have victory over the battles we have in our lives.

But in order to stand in that victory, we need to better understand who Jesus is and what He has won for us as our reigning King.

Before we study those truths, let's dwell in these ancient words of "A Mighty Fortress," written by Martin Luther around 1527. May these truths become our anthem song as we learn to truly live in our unshakable victory of Christ:

> A mighty fortress is our God,
> a bulwark never failing;
> our helper he, amid the flood
> of mortal ills prevailing.
> For still our ancient foe
> does seek to work us woe;
> his craft and power are great,
> and armed with cruel hate,
> on earth is not his equal.
>
> Did we in our own strength confide,
> our striving would be losing,
> were not the right Man on our side,
> the Man of God's own choosing.
> You ask who that may be?
> Christ Jesus, it is he;
> Lord Sabaoth his name,
> from age to age the same;
> and he must win the battle.
>
> And though this world, with devils filled,
> should threaten to undo us,
> we will not fear, for God has willed
> his truth to triumph through us.
> The prince of darkness grim,

we tremble not for him;
his rage we can endure,
for lo! his doom is sure;
one little word shall fell him.

That Word above all earthly powers
no thanks to them abideth;
the Spirit and the gifts are ours
through him who with us sideth.
Let goods and kindred go,
this mortal life also;
the body they may kill:
God's truth abideth still;
his kingdom is forever![6]

His Kingdom is Forever!

Pray this roar of victory with me.

Father God, we worship You as our Most High. You are our mighty fortress and Your kingdom is forever. Thank You for sending Your beloved Son to die in my place to conquer sin, death, and the evil one. Teach me how to live in that victory every day and to never take for granted all that Jesus endured to secure that victory. In Your holy and mighty name, I pray. Amen.

The Roar of His Word:

Read Ephesians 6:10–13.

Worship Song:

"A Mighty Fortress," as sung by Tommy Bailey and Keith and Kristyn Getty.[7]

chapter two

THE REIGNING KING

He is the radiance of the glory of God and the exact imprint
  of his nature,
and he upholds the universe by the word of his power.
After making purification for sins,
he sat down at the right hand of the Majesty on high.

HEBREWS 1:3

MY BELOVED MOTHER battled Alzheimer's for the last fourteen years of her life until God took her home at the age of eighty-four. She loved Jesus probably more than anyone else I have ever known. Her unwavering faith in Him shone brightly, even in the terrifying fog of Alzheimer's as it tried to steal her memories and her dignity.

A few years before her death, I was straightening up some clutter in my parents' room and I found a yellow sticky note on a pile of old newspapers. I am surprised I didn't just toss the papers, but thankfully my mother's beautiful handwriting caught my eye—handwriting that had long since disappeared due to her Alzheimer's.

The note said, "I'm fading away, but Jesus is keeping me every day."

Under that declaration of her deep faith while enduring deep sorrow, she also wrote "Hebrews 12:1–2." Years later I was able to trace those words in her handwriting onto a painted yellow canvas. This reminder now sits in my window by my writing desk.

After my mother's death, I found another sticky note tucked in the front of her Bible where she had again written "Hebrews 12:1–2."

I call that my sticky note legacy.

Those verses proclaim:

> Therefore, since we are surrounded by so great a cloud of witnesses, let us also lay aside every weight, and sin which clings so closely, and let us run with endurance the race that is set before us, looking to Jesus, the founder and perfecter of our faith, who for the joy that was set before him endured the cross, despising the shame, and is seated at the right hand of the throne of God.

Though I can't think of anything much worse than losing your mind to Alzheimer's, my mother still fixed her eyes (and heart) on Jesus, her risen and ascended Savior, right up until the end of her life. We were amazed that she could still sing a few lines of her favorite hymns even when she no longer spoke or recognized us.

I assume that most of you picking up this book have your own deep sorrows or trials you are facing now, or have in the recent past. Life is hard. Your problems are real—mine too. So often this earthly life can eclipse our view of our triumphant King Jesus who is seated at the right hand of the throne of God. It's hard to keep our eyes fixed on Him and the truth of His Word when sorrow or trials rage. As a woman serving in Christian ministry for years—who has also battled fear, anxiety, and the near destruction of my marriage—I've tried to learn to fix my eyes and heart upward where Jesus sits at the right hand of God as our reigning and victorious King.

AT THE RIGHT HAND
OF THE THRONE OF GOD

In order to put our trust in God for our protection and victory, we need to know deep down in our souls that He is truly our Victor. Have you ever considered what it means that Jesus ascended and sits at the right hand of the throne of God and how that applies to our here and now, everyday lives? Let's turn our eyes together to our ascended King.

We can only imagine the celebration of the angels once Jesus was finally back in their midst after He ascended from earth and "sat down at the right hand of the Majesty on high" (Hebrews 1:3). What awe and wonder there must have been when He sat down at the right hand of the throne of God, signifying that His work on earth was finished, death had been defeated, and He was home!

Have you ever considered what it means that Jesus ascended and sits at the right hand of the throne of God and how that applies to our here and now, everyday lives?

Did shouts of praise, songs of adoration, even tears of joy fill the heavenly realms as He took His seat? (I know we are told in Scripture that there will be no tears in heaven, but I like to think tears of joy will be there, as that is one of the most beautiful of all human emotions, don't you think?)[1]

Jesus Christ's position of authority and victory at the right hand of the Father was purchased through the excruciating death and victorious resurrection *and* through the glorious ascension of our Savior. So often most of the teaching we hear in our churches or Bible studies focuses on the sacrificial earthly life and death of Christ and His resurrection—all essentials of our Christian faith. But we often overlook or diminish what Jesus Christ accomplished through His ascension to the right hand of His Father.

I see the ascension of Christ as the crescendo of His "It is finished!" victory cry from the cross. After His death and resurrection, and after forty days with His beloved disciples, Jesus ascended to heaven and *sat down* at the right hand of the throne of God. I love how Darrell Bock, a seminary research professor, describes the ascension of Christ: "The ascension is not just a departure; it is also an arrival."[2]

Bible teacher Christine Gordon describes this glorious scene:

> When he stands in the presence of God and takes his place on the throne, he represents all who are redeemed, therefore giving us access to the throne room. The ascension is not an afterthought or a way to wrap up the story. The ascension is the coronation of the king, the finishing of his work, the beginning of his heavenly reign and of his giving of gifts to the church. The true triumphal entry happened when the King of Kings, having accomplished his work on earth, returned to heaven as the exalted king.[3]

But what does this heavenly reign mean to us today? Do we imagine Jesus there as if He's just waiting to return one day? What is He currently doing?

Too often when we read the gospel account of the ascension in Luke, we think of it only as an ending to the earthly ministry of Christ, almost as if He is deserting His beloved disciples right when they are finally understanding who He is and need Him the most. Instead, it is the triumphal entry of the King, as Gordon so eloquently describes it. And, as we see at the closing of the book of Luke, this moment is a sending out of the disciples to carry the gospel to the world:

> "You are witnesses of these things. And behold, I am sending the promise of my Father upon you. But stay in the city until you are clothed with power from on high."

And he led them out as far as Bethany, and lifting up his hands he blessed them. While he blessed them, he parted from them and was carried up into heaven. And they worshiped him and returned to Jerusalem with great joy, and were continually in the temple blessing God. (Luke 24:48–53)

The Bible speaks often about the "right hand of God," but what does that really mean? We see in Scripture that the right hand of God is used as a symbol of God's power, His protection, and His presence, but also of His judgment. And it is a symbol of His triumphant victory and the defeat of God's enemies.[4]

The powerful word picture of "the right hand of God" is mentioned many times in the Old Testament. The Psalms provide particularly stunning references in the context of God's sovereign protection and power at His right hand (see Psalms 16:8; 63:8; 89:13; 139:10, to name just a few).

In Exodus 15:6, we're told, "Your right hand, O LORD, glorious in power, your right hand, O LORD, shatters the enemy."

Oh, how we need to know what shatters the enemy!

King David prophesied about this position of Christ, long before the birth of his Messiah: "The LORD says to my Lord: 'Sit at my right hand, until I make your enemies your footstool'" (Psalm 110:1). Jesus even quoted this psalm as He defended His position as the Son of God before the religious leaders of the day (see Luke 20:42).

The New Testament repeatedly uses this phrase as well, but in reference to the position of authority held by the resurrected and ascended Christ. In Ephesians 1:21, we are told that Jesus is "above all rule and authority and power and dominion, and above every name that is named, not only in this age but also in the one to come." In fact, Jesus Himself proclaimed His seated position at the right hand of God while He was under arrest and facing His crucifixion!

> When day came, the assembly of the elders of the people gathered together, both chief priests and scribes. And they led him away to their council, and they said, "If you are the Christ, tell us." But he said to them, "If I tell you, you will not believe, and if I ask you, you will not answer. But *from now on* the Son of Man *shall be seated at the right hand of the power of God.*" (Luke 22:66–69)

From now on!

Let that sink in if you find yourself questioning His power and position of authority when this earthly life rages over you. Let that sink in when your friends or family try to sway you away from your faith in the risen and reigning Jesus.

Those Scriptures shout the truth of the victory, power, and authority of our Lord Jesus, and we have all of that same victory, power, and authority because we are His. Said another way:

> We do not fight for victory; we fight from victory. We do not fight in order to win but because in Christ we have already won. Overcomers are those who rest in the victory already given to them by their God.[5]

Don't you love that? Because of Jesus Christ, we do not need to "fight *for* victory; we fight *from* victory!" *In* Christ, we have already won!

Oh, yes, the battles will continue to rage as we walk through this earthly life. But we must learn to cling to the truth that we are not fighting *for* victory, but we are fighting *from* victory. When the battles and storms of life hit us hard (and they will), may we remember and cling to the truth that our Lord Jesus has triumphed over the evil one: "Having disarmed the powers and authorities, he made a public spectacle of them, triumphing over them by the cross" (Colossians 2:15 NIV).

He has triumphed! He has won! He is the Victor! He is greater than the evil one who roars! Let's not believe the lie that the enemy has more power or influence than our God. First John 4:4 reminds us: "Little children, you are from God and have overcome them, for he who is in you is greater than he who is in the world."

That is our victory cry. That is our victory roar.

Remember Liam's lion and the protective barrier that guarded him? It's so easy to forget that Jesus is our protective barrier and instead to believe we are on our own. I think it's helpful if we ask ourselves these questions:

> Do I stand, fight, and rest in the victory that Jesus Christ, the Lion of Judah, has purchased for me?
>
> Or, do I often live defeated and afraid as if the enemy has more power and the louder roar than my triune God?

Yes, the enemy has power on this earth right now, but his future is the lake of fire.[6]

Because of Jesus, we can be mighty warriors who live in victory, and thankfully, we are not in this battle alone.

WHAT IS JESUS DOING NOW AT THE RIGHT HAND OF GOD?

We've been looking at what it means that Jesus is seated at the right hand of God in terms of His authority over the evil one and our victory in Christ, but it's easy to wonder what Jesus is doing now in that position. When deep sorrows hit us, we can forget that Jesus is seated at the right hand of the throne of God with full authority over our world, sin, and the devil. As waves of trials and tragedies come, we can doubt if our God is in control, or if He even cares or is aware of our suffering. We can fall into the trap of thinking that God is cold and distant, too busy or uninterested to care about us. It is easy for us to go there in our minds—questioning God's goodness and presence—especially when the storms of life assail us. But, remember: our God walks on water.

The psalmist David often describes our water-walking God who rescues His beloved in the storms. Tucked away in Psalm 18:16 we're told that, "He reached down from on high and took hold of me; he drew me out of deep waters" (NIV). I often tear up when I read those words because it reminds me of His rescue of me during a devastating time in my life. This all-powerful, holy, magnificent God has cared enough about the storms of my life to reach down from on high, take hold of me, and draw me out of the deep waters.

When I first discovered this verse, I pictured my God walking or even running on the waves of my stormy life to get to me, reaching down with powerful arms and hands and pulling me out of the raging sea.

Oh, seaweed was still wrapped around my feet, the storm was still raging, I was gasping for air . . . but He had come for me, He took hold of me and His presence began to calm the storm in my heart and mind. I think that is what the disciples saw as well as Jesus pushed through the stormy seas to walk on water to get to them. I don't think He looked like the Jesus of my childhood flannelgraph stories in Sunday school in the sixties, where the same cutout figure of Jesus was used for every scene in those stories. So, when He confronted the Pharisees for their legalism, when He healed the sick, when He wept at a friend's grave and when He walked on the stormy seas, He had the same expression on His face as that cutout figure. His white robe was always spotless and never wrinkled, His hands were folded in kind of a wimpy way, and every hair was in place.

Well, that might have been the Jesus in those flannelgraph stories. But that is not the Jesus of the New Testament or the God that

I have come to know. Instead, most likely while lightning flashed around Him and the waves and wind threatened to overtake Him, there was relentless determination on His face as He walked on the stormy seas to get to His disciples. And I think He just might have that same expression on His face as He treads the stormy waves of our own stories, reaching down from on high and drawing us out of the consuming waves.

Are you struggling with wondering if Jesus is even aware of what you are going through? Do you sometimes think of Him as an uncaring and distant God? That is where the enemy wants to take us in our thinking. Let's choose together instead to hold on to the promise we are given in God's Word that "Christ Jesus is the one who died—more than that, who was raised—*who is at the right hand of God, who indeed is interceding for us*" (Romans 8:34).

Read that again: Christ Jesus *is interceding for us.* In all of His power and glory and majesty, Jesus is still praying *for us* . . . at the right hand of God!

In his book *Gentle and Lowly: The Heart of Christ for Sinners and Sufferers*, author Dane Ortlund devotes a whole chapter to what it means that Christ is interceding for us. He begins the chapter with this powerful teaching:

> When we talk about Christ's intercession, we are talking about what Jesus is doing *now.* There has been a remarkable recovery of the glory of what Christ did *back then,* in his life, death, and resurrection, to save me. But what about what he is doing now? For many of us, our functional Jesus isn't really doing anything now; everything we need to be saved, we tend to think, is already accomplished.[7]

Ortlund continues with the awe and wonder of the truth that Jesus is constantly interceding for us:

It isn't as if his heart throbbed for his people when he was on earth but has dissipated now that he is in heaven. It's not that his heart was flowing forth in a burst of mercy that took him all the way to the cross but has now cooled down, settling back once more into kindly indifference. His heart is as drawn to his people now as ever it was in his incarnate state. *And the present manifestation of his heart for his people is his constant interceding on their behalf.*[8]

When I first read that in Ortlund's book, I highlighted that paragraph and then wrote in the margin "Thank You, Lord Jesus! Help me remember this truth!" How often do we wonder if His heart has grown indifferent toward us?

Not only is Jesus interceding to the Father on our behalf, we are promised in that same chapter in Romans that the Holy Spirit groans in prayer for us:

> Likewise the Spirit helps us in our weakness. For we do not know what to pray for as we ought, *but the Spirit himself intercedes for us with groanings too deep for words.* And he who searches hearts knows what is the mind of the Spirit, because *the Spirit intercedes for the saints according to the will of God.* (Romans 8:26–27)

Have you ever been in a place in your life where you can't find the words to pray? Where the sorrows are so deep that your soul is groaning? I know I have. In those times, knowing that the Holy Spirit "intercedes for us with groanings too deep for words" has brought me much comfort and hope. Those groanings are part of God's roar over us when we need Him the most.

Not only are we promised that Jesus is at the right hand of God, we are also promised in God's Word that we are seated there *with*

Him in the "heavenly places in Christ Jesus" (Ephesians 2:6). I used to think that was only in our future, when we were finally with Him in heaven. But in her book *Seated with Christ,* author Heather Holleman teaches what it means that we are seated with Christ in the heavenly places . . . today.

> We know that we will enter into heaven when we physically die, but there's also a sense that some part of the kingdom of heaven has already begun in us right now. The kingdom of God, like our seat in the heavenly realms, will come about in fullness as we enter heaven, but as believers, we are at this very moment part of God's kingdom and seated with Christ.[9]

Let those truths be your compass as you navigate the often stormy seas that threaten to take you under. Even in pandemics, cancer, infertility, job loss, betrayal, and other uncertainties, our Lord Jesus is seated and in control, and we are seated with Him.

The truth that we are seated with Christ and that the triune God intercedes—even groans—for us in prayer should take our breath away and send us to our knees in worship of Him. Let the roar of those promises from Romans 8 and Ephesians 2 encourage you right now.

> If you are like my dear childhood friend battling cancer . . . remember He intercedes for you.

> If you are grieving the death of a loved one like my sister-in-law Teresa, who lost both her parents within one week of each other due to the COVID-19 pandemic . . . remember He groans in prayer for you.

> If you are praying for a prodigal child like many I know . . . remember He intercedes for your child.

If it seems like Jesus is a distant God . . . remember you are seated with Him.

Going back to Romans 8:34 one more time, do you see how that verse emphasizes the death, resurrection *and* ascension of Jesus: "Christ Jesus is the one *who died*—more than that, *who was raised—who is at the right hand of God*, who indeed is *interceding for us.*"

Died. Raised. At the right hand of God. Interceding.

That is where our Lord Jesus is right now! As we go through this book together, may we fully, and finally, grasp what it means to keep our eyes on Jesus as the One who is seated at the right hand of the throne of God, now and forever. It is there where we can see more clearly what it means to stand (or sit) with Him in victory.

Pray this worship prayer with me:

Lord Jesus, forgive me for my diminished view of the power of Your death, resurrection, and ascension. Forgive me when I live as though I am defeated and as if the enemy has more power than You do. I worship You as the One who is seated at the right hand of the throne of God. When the roars of this world, my sin, and the enemy seem deafening, may I remember that You, Jesus, have the loudest roar over me! Thank You for all You endured to purchase my victory. Teach me what it means to stand and rest in that victory today, no matter what I am going through. I worship You as both the Lion of Judah and as the Lamb who sacrificed Your life for me. Today, I join the victory roar of Revelation 5, "To him who sits on the throne and to the Lamb be blessing and honor and glory and might forever and ever!" Jesus, You are worthy! You are seated! It is finished!

The Roar of His Word:

Read these verses as part of your prayer time with Him or for further study: Hebrews 12:1–2; Ephesians 2:4–10; Romans 8:26–28, 34.

Worship Songs:

"Is He Worthy?"[10] sung by Andrew Peterson.

chapter three

GOD WITH US

For thus says the One who is high and lifted up,
   who inhabits eternity, whose name is Holy:
"I dwell in the high and holy place,
   and also with him who is of a contrite and lowly spirit,
to revive the spirit of the lowly,
   and to revive the heart of the contrite."

ISAIAH 57:15

A YEAR BEFORE she started medical school at Michigan State, our daughter Christie worked at a medical clinic for almost six months in West Africa in the country of Côte d'Ivoire (known as the Ivory Coast). She lived with a local family who welcomed her as their own. While there, Christie helped deliver babies, triaged patients in the walk-in clinic, and worked in the HIV/AIDS community outreach and education clinic. She would tell you that God used her time in West Africa to confirm His calling on her life to be a doctor.

After she came back home just before Christmas, she soon shared a story with us about her last week in Côte d'Ivoire that would have terrified me if I had heard it while she was still living there. One morning, on her usual route to work, she passed through a security checkpoint that was more heavily lined with armed guards than usual. In a country recovering in the aftermath of civil war, security checkpoints weren't outside the norm; but this time, something was different— the usual policemen had been replaced with armed military guards. One of the new guards stopped her and demanded to see her passport. Still a novice speaker of French (the national language), Christie showed her papers but couldn't understand the rapid-fire commands that followed. After a brief confrontation, the disgruntled guard finally waved her through the checkpoint, and she was able to go on to the clinic where she worked.

Once she arrived there, Christie shared with the other medical staff what had happened. The concern on their faces signaled she would not be safe to travel that path back home in the evening, at least not alone. After work that day, a small brigade of Ivorian family members and colleagues left the clinic compound on their motorcycles with Christie at the helm on her own motorbike. She was the first by several minutes to pull up to the checkpoint. The same military guard stood armed and looming over the draw bridge gate, a look of disdain on his face.

It was obvious from his expression that he was not satisfied with the outcome of their prior confrontation. Suddenly, more guards appeared. The guard demanded she follow him to a different room for questioning, something she knew she absolutely should not do. She felt cornered, and despite the help she knew followed her, utterly alone. Within minutes, the cavalry descended. She was surrounded by her own guard of Ivorian uncles and brothers, armed with their knowledge of the local laws and at the ready to defend her. One of them got off his bike, walked up to the guard, and confronted him to his face, telling him he had no right to question or threaten Christie since she had the right documents to pass unencumbered through the checkpoint. No longer alone and vulnerable, Christie was allowed to pass through to safety.

When Christie first told me that story, I thought it was such a picture of our Savior's protection over us. Often, we think we are on our own, vulnerable to the enemy's attacks, lies, and accusations, when all the while Jesus and His army of angels are surrounding and covering us, hemming us in from all sides. Because we are His and He has purchased our victory over the evil one and his minions, we do not need to be afraid. We can stand strong and courageous against the enemy's attacks because Jesus is forever with us as Immanuel, our "God with us."

There have been seasons in my life where I have had a diminished sense or awareness of God's presence and powerful protection over me. Often, we bring God down to our level, relegating Him to a God who is intent primarily on making us comfortable, happy, and content with this earthly life. Then, when trials or temptations rain down on us, or reign over us, we question His goodness and mercy—or even His sovereignty and protection over us.

I remember a time when I was precariously on the edge of turning my heart away from trusting God due to severe trials. I'll share more about the circumstances later in the book, but I can testify that in His lovingkindness God reached my questioning, fragile heart with a familiar Bible story I had read many times. It's a story of a man who has become one of my greatest heroes of the faith; a man who had every reason to leave his faith in Christ, yet stood strong until the end.

This story demonstrates how Jesus is ever aware and interceding for us, never leaving or forsaking us—even in our darkest hour.

The hero's name is Stephen.

STANDING OVATION

Just moments before Stephen's death, God peeled back the curtain of heaven to give this devoted follower of Christ a glimpse of where he was headed. The raging crowd was intent on killing Stephen, the first recorded martyr of the early church. As Stephen was being stoned, he looked up and saw Jesus *standing* at His Father's side:

> But he, full of the Holy Spirit, gazed into heaven and saw the glory of God, and Jesus standing at the right hand of God. And he said, "Behold, I see the heavens opened, and the Son of Man standing at the right hand of God." (Acts 7:55–56)

It was as if Jesus stood in Stephen's honor, letting him know He was right there waiting for him.

We are given only a brief glimpse of Stephen's life in Acts, chapters 6–8. Stephen's main calling was to care for the needs of widows, serving them food (6:1–3). That seems like a humble calling while other apostles were called to lead the early church through what seems like more significant roles (v. 4). Yet, I believe that the impact of Stephen's life—and especially his death—was the key catalyst for the early church's explosive growth.

We're told in Acts 6:5 that Stephen was "a man full of faith and of the Holy Spirit" and in verse 8 that he was "full of grace and power . . . doing great wonders and signs among the people." Imagine your life being described like that in God's Word! Stephen was a gifted teacher, and he became a threat to the spiritual leaders of the day, to the point that false witnesses rose up against him, claiming they "heard him speak blasphemous words against Moses and God" (v. 11).

In this dramatic scene where Stephen was being accused and was under the threat of arrest—and even death—we're told that his face was like the face of an angel as he boldly defended his faith (Acts 7). Push pause, read that chapter, and try to picture the scene as if you're in the crowd listening to Stephen's words. Stephen spoke of the steadfast faith of those who had gone before him, recounting the stories of Abraham, Isaac, and Jacob, and on to Joseph, Moses, Joshua, King

David, and King Solomon. Stephen then quotes from the prophet Isaiah: "Heaven is my throne, and the earth is my footstool" (Acts 7:49; see Isaiah 66:1).

After quoting those ancient words, Stephen's boldness crescendoed to a mighty roar in verses 51–53 where he condemned his accusers. That enraged the crowd. As I read that scene, it seems that at one moment the crowd must have looked like schoolyard bullies with gnashing teeth and rocks in hand, then the next like monstrous demons being let loose from hell to kill an innocent man.

But even in such terror, Stephen sees Jesus standing at the right hand of God. And he announces this to all present . . . and to us today.

How stunning that after Stephen quoted from the prophet Isaiah, proclaiming "Heaven is my throne, and the earth is my footstool" God rolled back the curtain of heaven, showing Stephen that magnificent scene just moments before his death.

Indeed, this earth is God's footstool!

Stephen tried to get the raging crowd to look up to see the heavenly scene opened for him, but instead they covered their ears and rushed at him to stone him to death.

Even while Stephen was dying, he cried out for God to forgive his murderers.

> And as they were stoning Stephen, he called out, "Lord Jesus, receive my spirit." And falling to his knees he cried out with a loud voice, "Lord, do not hold this sin against them." And when he had said this, he fell asleep. (Acts 7:59–60)

Can you imagine?

Oh, how much Stephen's heart was like the heart of his Lord Jesus who groaned similar words as He was dying on a cross—for that same crowd, for Stephen, and for you and me.

How could anyone watching Stephen's death ever be the same? I wonder if his dying words of forgiveness echoed in the ears of his murderers, as they walked away from Stephen's broken body.

One of the most significant figures witnessing Stephen's death was Saul (later known also as Paul). In Acts 7:58, we see the crowd laying "down their garments at the feet of a young man named Saul." It seems that this was as an act of showing respect and honor to Saul and his leadership, as if they were saying that they were killing Stephen in Saul's honor.

Acts 8 opens with these shocking words. "And Saul approved of his execution."

We are then told what transpired after this: "And there arose on that day a great persecution against the church in Jerusalem, and they were all scattered throughout the regions of Judea and Samaria, except the apostles. Devout men buried Stephen and made great lamentation over him. But Saul was ravaging the church, and entering house after house, he dragged off men and women and committed them to prison" (Acts 8:1b–3).

You almost sense a battle in the heavenlies after Stephen's murder as Saul ravaged the church, dragging men and women out of their homes and throwing them into prison. To the Christians, it must have seemed like all was lost and that the enemy had triumphed. Instead, as only our God can do, that persecution and suffering actually birthed the growth of the early church as believers scattered after Stephen's death, taking the good news of Jesus with them.

And what about Saul? Though he was on a rampage to persecute Christians, I suspect he couldn't shake what he saw and heard as brave Stephen died in front of him. How could a man ever forget such a scene? Perhaps that is part of the reason Saul listened to the One who blinded him with truth when he was confronted on a dusty road not long after Stephen's murder. Perhaps Stephen's last words also echoed in Paul's heart when he later had to endure his own chains, prisons, and beatings.

Not all martyrs die like Stephen—with the glow of glory on their face and witnesses to canonize their courage. Some pass quickly in the night or alone in a prison, some in fiery explosions or crowded camps. I can't help but wonder if all who die for following Christ meet a standing Savior, welcoming them home.

This glimpse of God opening the heavens to His throne room for Stephen in his darkest hour is such a beautiful illustration of Isaiah 57:15: "For thus says the One who is high and lifted up, who inhabits eternity, whose name is Holy: 'I dwell in the high and holy place, and also with him who is of a contrite and lowly spirit, to revive the spirit of the lowly, and to revive the heart of the contrite.'"

If you are navigating deep trials, or if you sense that your own sin or the enemy are winning the battles you are facing, cling to the truth that:

> Our high and lifted up God . . .
>> Who inhabits eternity . . .
>>> Whose name is Holy . . .
>>>> Who dwells in the high and holy place . . .
>>>>> also *dwells* with us—to revive our lowly spirits and contrite hearts.

Our God, *who inhabits eternity, whose name is Holy . . . dwells* with us!

Stephen's story promises us that.

Paul's story promises us that.

My mom's Alzheimer's story promises us that. Remember, she knew that "though she was fading away, Jesus was keeping her every day."

When your own life seems filled with heartache and pain, defeat or disaster—remember He keeps you. He defends you. He guards you. He protects you. He is the High and Lofty One who dwells with you.

One of the most significant times in my walk with Christ was when I was in my early twenties and I moved to Vienna, Austria, to work for a ministry where pastors and seminary professors were writing biblical curriculum to train and equip pastors who lived under Communism in Eastern Europe. In the early eighties I traveled from Vienna to Bucharest, Romania, where I smuggled in the curriculum for pastors who would be teaching the material to other pastors in the underground church. At that time, they could not go to seminary or even freely preach the truth of the gospel without the threat of being arrested, beaten, or even killed.

The country was ruled by the tyrannical dictator Nicolae Ceauşescu, who was often likened to Stalin because of his brutality in persecuting the people of Romania, especially Christians. During my short stay in Bucharest, I met with a pastor and his young family who were sacrificing so much just to share the hope of Christ with others. Their courage made a deep impression on me as a young woman; I often took for granted the freedoms I had to go to church and study the Bible with others.

Some of the pastors I worked with in Romania often taught at one of the hidden churches in the countryside. They shared how the room was filled with people, packed in like sardines, where they sang in hushed voices and lingered for hours just to hear the teaching and to worship together. They were a people who knew that God was not only high and lifted up, but also with them in the darkness and oppression of Communism.

Revival came to the church in Romania through suffering, much like the early church in Acts. By the close of that decade—on Christmas Day 1989—the hold of Communism on Romania finally crumbled. The revolution was marked by courageous people standing for freedom, including college students who risked their lives while surrounding a church in peaceful protest when the military police came.

I share that story as an example of how the God who stood in Stephen's honor still stands with His followers today in our own suffering. You may never have to go through the type of persecution Stephen did or what Christians are enduring under Communism. But many of you have been through deep sorrow that has threatened to overtake you or make you question your faith in Him. There is a battle raging over many believers right now to leave their faith and not finish the race that has been marked out for them. I believe that is one of the enemy's most strategic tactics today.

Remember: just as Jesus stood for Stephen in His pain, He is ever aware of our suffering and enters into it with us.

Did you notice how Stephen—even while his life was being threatened—gave such honor and reverence to his God? His story shows us the balance of a high view of God—one filled with reverence and a holy fear of Him—coupled with the Immanuel, God *with* us, heart of our Savior. I assume Stephen didn't fully understand God's decision for his life to end that abruptly and in such a brutal way. For some reason, God chose martyrdom for Stephen's life, while bringing new life and a holy calling to Paul's life soon after.

I'm not sure I'll ever understand, this side of eternity, how God makes those decisions. But one thing I know: God used Stephen's story to recapture my heart and bring me back to the truth that our God reigns, that He is sovereign, and that He is ever aware of what we are facing on this groaning earth.

> **Remember: just as Jesus stood for Stephen in His pain, He is ever aware of our suffering and enters into it with us.**

May we never choose to leave Him because the Christian life gets too hard or asks too much.

Will you pray this prayer of surrender with me?

Father God, thank You for opening the heavens for Stephen in his darkest hour, which became his most triumphant hour. What a beautiful example of how he fixed his eyes on You as the battle raged around him. May I have a heart like his, a heart that knows Your Word, a heart that loves You above all else—even life itself. Thank You that while You dwell in the high and holy place, You also dwell with us as our Immanuel—our God who is *with* us. Awaken and revive my heart and mind to Your power and majesty, authority and dominion. I bow to You in worship. You are the One who is high and lifted up . . . the One who inhabits eternity . . . the One whose name is Holy, Holy, Holy. Turn my eyes upon You. Teach me what it means to honor You, to fear You, to trust You, to worship You in the beauty of Your holiness—no matter what I am facing. In Your mighty and powerful, yet personal name, I pray. Amen.

The Roar of His Word:

Read these verses aloud as part of your prayer time with Him or for further study: Isaiah 57:15; Hebrews 2:5–18.

Worship Song:

"He Will Hold Me Fast" sung by Shane & Shane.[1]

We've looked at how God hemming us in with His protection helps us stand firm. Next, we will learn how it is only because of Him that we can stand in that victory every day, especially in the battles we have with fear, temptation, and doubts and lies about our God that we believe. Thankfully, our God has provided all that we need to finish the race He has marked out for us in victory. We do not have to live in defeat or discouragement or go through our battles in our own strength. Jesus is our armor of protection. Because of Him, and only because of Him, we can stand firmly and confidently and securely in that protection.

part two

HIS UNSHAKABLE VICTORY

Then shall my hand never weaken,

my feet never stumble,

my sword never rest,

my shield never rust,

my helmet never shatter,

my breastplate never fall,

as my strength rests in the power of thy might.

A PURITAN PRAYER
THE VALLEY OF VISION[1]

chapter four

WHEN I AM AFRAID

Fear not, for I have redeemed you;
  I have called you by name, you are mine.
When you pass through the waters, I will be with you;
  and through the rivers, they shall not overwhelm you;
when you walk through fire you shall not be burned,
  and the flame shall not consume you.
For I am the LORD your God,
  the Holy One of Israel, your Savior.

ISAIAH 43:1-3

I'VE BATTLED ANXIETY for much of my life. There have been seasons in which I experienced the normal worries of motherhood, such as concern for toddlers with high fevers or settling our children into new schools because of our many moves. But there have been other seasons where I thought my anxiety would take me under.

You may not battle anxiety and fear; but perhaps you are battling something else where the enemy has learned you are most vulnerable and where he tries to defeat you. In Part One, we focused on Jesus as our reigning, interceding Savior who dwells with us and who has won an unshakable victory. But what happens in the actual day-to-day experience of living victoriously over something like fear (or wherever he attacks you the most)?

I believe that some of my tendency toward anxiety is how I am wired and that I will have to continuously surrender my worries to Jesus throughout my life. But there have been times when I know that the enemy targets the areas where I am most vulnerable, trying to defeat me and make me question God's presence and protection over me and my family.

One of those seasons of fear was during our move to Beijing when our daughters were only three and five years old.

The famous opening line to Charles Dickens's novel *A Tale of Two Cities* aptly describes our three years in China: "It was the best of times, it was the worst of times."[2] Some of our best times were when we'd explore that fascinating city. I especially remember one autumn day when we caravanned with a few other families to a remote part of the Great Wall in our cars, Jeeps, and sidecar motorcycles. To make it even more of an adventure, we decided to bring our tents so we could camp on the Wall that night. My husband, Rick, drove our antique sidecar motorcycle with our two little girls and their lop-eared rabbit, Moses, tucked in the sidecar. I followed behind in our Jeep, loaded with our cooler of food.

Arriving at our favorite portion of the Great Wall—free from crowds and tourists—Rick pitched our tents while the girls and I climbed the steep stairs leading to a section that resembled the remnant of a castle. This part of the Wall was surrounded by a high and strong rampart, which once formed a defensive boundary.

Our younger daughter, Kelly, pretended to be a princess twirling 'round and 'round in her castle; her big sister Christie climbed the stairs to a high tower she wanted to explore. Later that night, as the sun began to set, we grilled chicken wings and roasted marshmallows for s'mores. Moses hopped around until the harvest moon illuminated the outline of the Wall, winding toward the horizon as far as our eyes could see.

Though it's a memory we will never forget—and it might sound like a magical, storybook life—our three years in China were actually some of the hardest years on our family. Kelly, tiny for her age, contracted many strange illnesses. While her body battled sickness, my heart battled the fear that often drove me to the point of panic. Rick's job was extremely stressful, and just navigating the traffic in Beijing made me wonder if he'd make it home alive after work. The enemy was also stepping up his attacks on me. In addition to the escalating fear for my children's safety, I fought a rising bitterness over having to live on the other side of the world. There were days I thought that he would win and days that I let him win, giving in to his lies about God's goodness and protection over us.

Years later, when our family was long settled back in the States, I found the photos from our camping trip on the Great Wall. One pictured our two small tents right in front of a portion of the Wall that included ramparts, strong towers, and shelters towering over the tents. Looking at that picture, I realized that for most of my time in China— and sadly much of my young adult life—I lived like someone in a tent, fearful and vulnerable to the storms and attacks on my family and me that could sweep us away. Yet, all along we were covered by our God who is our strong tower, shelter, and hiding place.

That is often how we—even as sons and daughters of the King— live our lives due to the attacks and lies the enemy hurls at us.

Even though we know deep down that our God reigns and His victory is ours, we often live defeated—consumed with fear, temptation, doubt, resentment, or bitterness—as the powers of darkness target our ministries, marriages, and families.

HEMMED IN

In the months leading up to moving to China, I was often filled with fear about moving there with our girls being so young. Before we left the States, they had to have many vaccines to protect them from mosquito-borne encephalitis and other potential diseases. That alone made me fearful, and neither of our preschool-aged daughters appreciated getting those painful shots.

One comfort to all of us was a children's CD of songs by Steve Green called *Hide 'Em in Your Heart* that we often listened to in our car.[3] This was a beautiful way for our little girls to memorize Bible verses, but God also used the lyrics to calm this mama's anxious heart as we prepared to move across an ocean. My favorite song, "When I Am Afraid," was based on Psalm 56:3–4. (You can still find it on YouTube, and listen to it after all these years.) I'll never forget my little girls in the back seat of the car singing that song at the top of their lungs while my eyes filled with hopeful tears that God saw us and was moving to China with us. These are the lyrics, directly taken from Scripture. Let the truths of these words bring you hope for your own fearful circumstances:

> *When I am afraid,*
> *I put my trust in you.*
> *In God, whose word I praise,*
> *in God I trust; I shall not be afraid.*
> *What can flesh to do me? (Psalm 56:3–4)*

If you read that psalm in your Bible, you'll see that David wrote those words when he was most likely filled with fear after being seized by the Philistines. He even tried to escape death in his own strength by feigning madness. You can read that story in 1 Samuel 21. I find it encouraging that a mighty warrior like David also battled fear, even resorting to a crazy tactic to try to protect himself.

EVEN THERE

Right after arriving in Beijing in the dead of winter of January 1995, the girls and I all came down with an upper respiratory illness, accompanied with fevers. It seemed as if all of my fears were coming true as we rushed one of our girls to the international clinic due to her high fever. On that drive, the lyrics to Psalm 56 kept playing through my mind . . . "when I am afraid, I put my trust in you . . . I shall not be afraid."

Another psalm I often clung to is Psalm 139, a stunning, lyrical song also written by David. This psalm is full of promises about our God's protective covering over us:

> You hem me in, behind and before,
>   and you lay your hand upon me.
> Such knowledge is too wonderful for me,
>   too lofty for me to attain . . .
> If I rise on the wings of the dawn,
>   if I settle on the far side of the sea,
> even there your hand will guide me,
>   your right hand will hold me fast. (vv. 5–6; 9–10 NIV)

Even there.

Even when our family literally moved to the far side of the sea, His hand held us fast and He truly hemmed us in from all sides. I couldn't always see it while we were living there, especially when our daughters were often dangerously ill. But looking back on those years, I know that is where Jesus began to forge my deep and abiding trust in Him, no matter the circumstances.

As followers of Christ, oh, that we would remember that no matter what we are facing, our God holds us fast and hems us in—even there. When you are battling fear or defeat in your life, picture Jesus hemming you in from all sides—He is above you, below you, on your left and your right. He hems you in from "behind and before," and He dwells within you through the Holy Spirit. You can't be any more covered in His protection than that: above, below, left and right, in front and behind—and within you!

> **Oh, that we would remember that no matter what we are facing, our God holds us fast and hems us in—even there.**

My father often told the story of growing up on a farm and one day finding a hen in a field that had died due to a prairie fire. When he gently moved her body aside with the toe of his boot, baby chicks scurried out from under her. He used that illustration to teach about God's protective covering over us in the fires of our lives. That is such a beautiful picture of being hemmed in from all sides and a great reminder when we feel alone, vulnerable, or fearful in the battles.

Our Immanuel—our *God with us*—doesn't promise that we won't have fires and storms in this life, but He does promise that He will be with us in those storms, never leaving or forsaking us. I recently read this quote from an interview with Dallas Jenkins, the director of the streaming series "The Chosen" on the life of Christ: "Jesus didn't come and change all the struggles people were having; he immersed himself in them."[4]

One of my favorite stories of how Jesus immerses Himself in the fires with us is found in Daniel 3. Though it's a familiar story, I encourage you to not skim over this part as it's a powerful picture of our Immanuel and how He enters into our trials (and battles) with us.

This story is about three brave young men (most likely teenagers) who refused to bow down and worship a golden image under the command of their king. The consequence of their courage would be a certain death by being thrown into a blazing, fiery furnace. But that didn't deter them in their stand against the king's edict. Right before they are thrown into the fire, one of them declares,

> "If we are thrown into the blazing furnace, the God we serve is able to deliver us from it, and he will deliver us from Your Majesty's hand. But even if he does not, we want you to know, Your Majesty, that we will not serve your gods or worship the image of gold you have set up." (Daniel 3:17–18 NIV)

What courage for such a young man to declare his "even if He does not" faith in his God. That enraged the king, and he had all three of the men tied up and thrown into the furnace. Moments later, we see one of the most stunning miracles recorded in Scripture. The king is astonished and says,

> "Look! I see four men walking around in the fire, unbound and unharmed, and the fourth looks like a son of the gods." Nebuchadnezzar then approached the opening of the blazing furnace and shouted, "Shadrach, Meshach and Abednego, servants of the Most High God, come out! Come here!" So Shadrach, Meshach and Abednego came out of the fire. (vv. 25–26 NIV)

I've read in many Bible commentaries that most likely that fourth man was Jesus—walking in the fire with the three men, rescuing them from death. The story ends with this proclamation from the king:

> "Praise be to the God of Shadrach, Meshach and Abednego, who has sent his angel and rescued his servants! They trusted in him and defied the king's command and were willing to give up their lives rather than serve or worship any god except their own God." (v. 28 NIV)

What are the "even there" or "even if" moments in your life when fear or sorrow threaten to consume you? May we borrow the courage of these three young men in our own fiery trials, knowing that Jesus is standing in the fire with us and hemming us in from all sides.

I recently heard about a Sunday school teacher who asked her class why Daniel wasn't afraid when he was thrown into the lion's den, and one little girl said, "because the Lion of Judah was in there with him."[5]

Do you believe that for your own story? We are promised in Psalm 46:11 that "the LORD of hosts is with us; the God of Jacob is our fortress."

One of the most powerful pictures of how the Lion of Judah hems us in with His protection is through *His* armor as outlined in Ephesians 6:10–18. God's armor shouts the victory Jesus has won for us. Turn to Ephesians 6, starting with verse 10, and read this victory cry out loud:

> Finally, be strong *in* the Lord and *in* the strength of *his* might. Put on the whole *armor of God*, that you may be able to stand against the schemes of the devil. For we do not wrestle against flesh and blood, but against the rulers, against the authorities, against the cosmic powers over this present darkness, against the spiritual forces of evil in the heavenly places. Therefore take up the whole *armor of God*, that you may be able to withstand in the evil day, and having done all, to stand firm. (Ephesians 6:10–13)

Notice the emphasis I added. It is only *in His* strength and might that we can be strong and stand firm in the battle against the evil one. And the armor is *God's* armor that we put on. Throughout the rest of this book, we will look at how we can use the mighty "roars" of God's Word, His armor, and prayer as our secure defensive covering and offensive weapons in the battles we face.

Some believe that it is up to us to "pray on" our armor every day in order to be covered by His protection. I've heard people say, "I forgot to pray on my armor today, no wonder I'm so defeated," as if we aren't covered by the armor if we forget to pray it on. But, remember that our armor is Jesus. He is the one who covers us, and our protection is not dependent on the daily ebb and flow of our faith. We can wear our armor boldly and securely because of who Jesus is: He covers us with *His* salvation (helmet), *His* righteousness (breastplate), *His* truth (belt), *His* peace (shoes), *His* faithfulness (shield), and *His* living Word (sword of the Spirit). Our part is to live securely and confidently in that victory and covering every day.

After I shared these truths in a conference workshop, a woman came up to me the next morning and said she had never thought of the armor that way. She said she read those verses in Ephesians with new eyes that morning. Before, she had always thought that it was up to her own striving to have enough faith, enough righteousness, and enough peace that would cover her, rather than living in the truth that Jesus had purchased that all for us through His death and resurrection.

That took me back to our years in China, where I desperately clung to the promises in God's Word of His protection during an especially dark night of the soul.

Toward the end of our first year in Beijing, Kelly, then three years old, became extremely sick one week with a high fever and sore throat that would not go away. Kelly was prone to strep throat, but the doctor at the international clinic would not give her antibiotics because the rapid test for strep was negative. After two days, my mama bear instincts kicked in and I called my pediatrician back in the US at 3:00 a.m. my time, 3:00 p.m. his. The doctor got on the phone and said, "This is a first—a call from a mom in China!" Though he couldn't diagnose her from thousands of miles away, he encouraged me to get her on antibiotics just in case it was strep, which can be deadly if untreated.

The clinic wouldn't be open until five hours later and there was nothing like 24-hour urgent care clinics in China in 1995. The closest hospital was hours away, and Kelly was finally sleeping peacefully after the Tylenol kicked in. I knew I had to wait out the night.

I look back at those terrifying, middle-of-the-night hours in Beijing as a turning point in my life as a mom and in my walk with Christ. Fear escalated to the point where I caught a glimpse of what it must be like to lose your mind over worry. I knew I had to get a grip on my fear in order to take care of my child.

Finally—and I mean, finally—I cried out to God. I asked Him to rescue me from the dark fears that were taking me under. I imagined I had Kelly in my arms (though she was sleeping in her room down the hall), and I lifted her to Him in prayer. I told Him that I knew He loved Kelly even more than I did and that she was His. Truly HIS. I promised to trust Him, love Him, and follow Him—no matter what He chose for my baby girl's life.

And, thankfully, I meant it. Soon, that beyond our human understanding peace promised in Philippians 4 began to cover me, and I finally fell back to sleep. And, when 8:00 a.m. arrived, this mama bear was on the phone to the clinic, demanding antibiotics for her little girl.

Kelly is now thirty years old and the mother of our grandson William (Wim), whose name means "resolute protector." That beautifully describes God's protective covering of Kelly since she was a little girl. He truly has been her Resolute Protector.

I know that God could have chosen a different story for our Kelly in China that dark night, and I am forever grateful that her health was restored. But I have several friends who are moms with a different story. Their worst fears were realized, and they have beloved children now in heaven. These women have shown me that sometimes God saves us from our worst fears, but other times, He carries us when our fears become reality. Their faith and trust in God as their refuge in such deep sorrow are stories of hope for all of us.

Now as I look at that picture of our small tents pitched on the Great Wall of China, in front of a strong tower and rampart, it reminds me of these powerful words from the psalmist David when he encountered his own fearful circumstances:

> *The angel of the LORD encamps*
> *around those who fear him, and delivers them.*
> *Oh, taste and see that the LORD is good!*
> *Blessed is the man who takes refuge in him! (Psalm 34:7–8)*

And in Psalm 27:5–6, David proclaims:

> *For he will hide me in his shelter*
> *in the day of trouble;*
> *he will conceal me under the cover of his tent;*
> *he will lift me high upon a rock.*
> *And now my head shall be lifted up*
> *above my enemies all around me,*
> *and I will offer in his tent*
> *sacrifices with shouts of joy;*
> *I will sing and make melody to the LORD.*

Whatever you are facing today, read those verses aloud to stand in those truths. I am so grateful that the Lord and His angels encamp around us, hemming us in from all sides, even during the dark nights of our souls.

He encamps around Kim, who lost her three-year-old son to strep throat, and has now written a book for grieving moms that is helping to rescue those moms from despair.[6] He encamps around Danita, a military widow with two little girls, who has written a book to bring hope and light to others who have experienced the crushing loss of a loved one.[7] These women have chosen God as their "refuge and strength, a very present help in trouble" (Psalm 46:1) even in their shattering grief.

I asked Danita recently how she has known that God encamps around her and her little girls, even after the loss of her husband. I pray that her story gives you hope for your own story of deep grief or fear.

> The word "encamps" stirs up different memories for me. I think of when Dan and I were first married and he traveled all the time with the military. He was gone more than half the month, almost every month—both international traveling and stateside. It was hard to sleep at night without him. I remember talking to my reverend and his wife about the fears, and they said, "Danita, it seems when Dan's traveling away from home that you think you're not protected. But Dan's prayers for you still cover you, even if he's overseas." Leaning into that truth relieved a lot of anxiety.
>
> Later when Dan deployed, our two-year-old memorized Psalm 91 as we prayed it every night over my husband, trusting that angels camped around Daddy.
>
> Those early years taught me to trust God more. Since Dan died, I've had a sense that his prayers are still covering me and our children, and so are the prayers of so many others. That has given me an amazing amount of security and unexplainable peace. I know that there are angels surrounding our home as promised in Psalm 91:11: "He will command his angels concerning you to guard you in all your ways." Sometimes, as I fall asleep, I imagine angels at every door and window, standing guard. Maybe "imagine" isn't the right word.

Maybe I see those angels with eyes of faith because they are really there even if I can't "see" them.

Do you sense that our Lord Jesus is your ever-present help in your own sorrow or fear? Do you sense that Jesus and His host of angels encamp around you? If not, ask Him to confirm those truths in your heart and mind. He wants to be your refuge and strength, an ever-present help in trouble. He is our only hope for rescuing us from fear or despair.

Whether you're a parent of an ill child, have lost a spouse, or someone facing what feels like enemies on all sides, remember that your God treads the stormy seas to get to you. Even though it might not feel like it right now, He is covering you with *His* armor which is His truth, His righteousness, His salvation, His peace, His faithfulness and the promises from His Word, our mighty sword of the Spirit.

In her Bible study *The Armor of God,* author Priscilla Shirer writes: "Your armor is Yahweh's own armor—given as a gift and empowered by His Spirit to ensure victory."[8]

Imagine if we could live in that understanding every day, in every battle. As a follower of Christ, you are covered in the gift of "Yahweh's own armor . . . and empowered by His Spirit to ensure victory."

We can also rest in the truth that "each part of the armor is intimately related to the Person and work of Christ. As we put on the armor, we are in reality clothing ourselves with the protection of the Lord Jesus Christ."[9]

HEAD TO TOE

If, like me, you wrestle with fear, especially for your children, one way to calm those fears is to turn your worries into prayers on their behalf. When our girls were little and I'd try to surrender my fears for their safety or health to God—I'd often think of them as being covered in His armor of protection from head to toe as I prayed over them. (Does the armor come in toddler sizes?) I would pray, "Thank You, Jesus, that You protect Christie and Kelly from head to toe like your armor covers us." That would often calm my fears, and I'd have a sense of surrendering them into His care. I am continuing to do that today as I pray over their children now, our beloved grandchildren.

For those of us who battle anxiety or fear, I think the pieces of the armor that resonate the most are the helmet of salvation and the sandals of peace. It's as if He is covering us from head to toe: His helmet protects our minds from our escalating fearful thoughts, and His peace covers us so that we can walk in it, no matter our circumstances.

I recently discovered a beautiful lullaby song called "Head to Toe" by Christy Nockels on her album *Be Held: Lullabies for the Beloved*. She also calls that song "The Armor of God Song."[10] Listen to that song as a reminder that we truly are covered from head to toe in Yahweh's armor.

> **For those who battle anxiety or fear, His helmet of salvation protects our minds from our escalating fearful thoughts, and His peace covers us so that we can walk in it, no matter our circumstances.**

And if you need a reminder that He is the bigger lion in the midst of your escalating fears, cling to this promise: "Little children, you are from God and have overcome them, for he who is in you is greater than he who is in the world" (1 John 4:4).

Before we study more about the armor in the remaining chapters, let's thank God for His protective covering over us.

Pray this victory prayer with me:

Dear Lord Jesus, thank You that You hem me in from all sides and that You dwell in me through the Holy Spirit. May I rest and abide in Your protective shelter over me. When I am afraid for my loved ones, help me turn those fears into prayers on their behalf. Thank You that Your armor of Your salvation, righteousness, truth, faithfulness, and peace cover me from the top of my head to the tip of my toes. Teach me how to live and stand in that victorious covering every day. Calm my anxious heart with Your peace that goes beyond my human understanding. Remind me that You encamp around me and that You are my rampart, my shelter, my fortress, and my strong deliverer. In Your mighty and victorious name, I pray. Amen.

The Roar of His Word:

Read these victory passages, even out loud, to cement these truths in your heart and mind today, especially if you are battling fear: Psalm 27:3–6; Psalm 56:3–4; Psalm 46.

Worship Songs:

"Even If" sung by MercyMe.[11] "Rescue" sung by Lauren Daigle.[12]

chapter five

WHEN I AM TEMPTED

I will greatly rejoice in the LORD;
  my soul shall exult in my God,
for he has clothed me with the garments of salvation;
  he has covered me with the robe of righteousness,
as a bridegroom decks himself like a priest with a beautiful headdress,
  and as a bride adorns herself with her jewels.

ISAIAH 61:10

"THIS WASN'T SUPPOSED to be my story!"

Through angry tears, I cried out those words to my husband. They seemed to hang above us in our room like a dark cloud. Rick and I were walking through a hard season in our marriage—and on this particular night, I felt hopeless about our future together.

A few weeks before, Rick had taken me away for a long weekend so he could confess sin he had hidden in his life. He had just shared his story with my father and our pastor. Their counsel to involve only those who would play a role in our healing and restoration proved wise. To those couples willing to stay and fight for their marriages, we've passed that counsel along. Thankfully, both men were praying for us when Rick confessed to me on that weekend away.

That was almost twenty years ago, and we will soon celebrate our 40th anniversary. Together, Rick and I share some of our story in this chapter as a message of hope for you who are facing defeat and hopelessness because of the choices you've made in your past or are being tempted to make now. Satan wants nothing more than to defeat us, making us believe we are beyond redemption.

In the weeks that followed Rick's confession, we were in intense marriage counseling, but my resolve to fight for our marriage was tenuous at times. One night right before going to sleep, I said to Rick, "I married a good man. A man who loves Jesus. Our parents prayed since we were little that we'd marry God's best for us." That's when I said, "This wasn't supposed to be my story!" as if I was speaking more to God than to my husband.

At that time, the only way I could fall asleep was if I wore my headphones and listened to worship music, making myself focus on the lyrics instead of the details of our seemingly hopeless story. So, as my words—*this wasn't supposed to be my story*—lingered over us, I put on my headphones, turned up my music, and tried to fall asleep.

Moments later, an old hymn began to play that I hadn't thought of in years.

> *Blessed assurance, Jesus is mine!*
> *Oh, what a foretaste of glory divine!*
> *Heir of salvation, purchase of God,*
> *Born of His spirit, washed in His blood.*
> *This is my story, this is my song,*
> *Praising my Savior all the day long;*
> *This is my story, this is my song,*
> *Praising my Savior all the day long.*[1]

To this day, that remains one of the most significant times in my life. Through those lyrics, it was as if God "reached down from on high and took hold of me; he drew me out of the deep waters" (Psalm 18:16) that threatened to consume me, Rick, and our marriage. I was focusing on our hopeless story, but there was another story God was writing for us.

Through tears, I began to sing out loud as the song played over me: "*This is my story, this is my song.*" Rick reached out for me and we cried together as he held me close. We knew we had years of work ahead of us for our marriage to heal, but our God whispered hope over us that night through an old hymn written almost one hundred and fifty years ago. God was telling us that we were His "heirs of salvation, purchase of God, born of His spirit and washed in His blood." Rick's sins. My sins. Your sins. Our past, present, and future sins—all washed in the blood of the Lamb.

THE BREASTPLATE OF RIGHTEOUSNESS

The word righteousness is kind of heady, one of those "churchy" words we often hear but don't fully grasp the meaning or significance of. To be righteous is to "act in accord with divine or moral law: free from guilt or sin, morally right or justifiable."[2]

The only way we can ever be considered "free from guilt or sin, morally right or justifiable" is because of the righteousness of Jesus Christ. It is His righteousness that covers us like a breastplate as we wear His armor. For years, I thought it was up to me to be "righteous" in my own strength and that was what protected me. But God's Word tells us in Titus 3:4–7:

> When the kindness and love of God our Savior appeared,
> he saved us, *not because of righteous things we had done,* but
> because of his mercy. He saved us through the washing of re-
> birth and renewal by the Holy Spirit, whom he poured out on
> us generously through Jesus Christ our Savior, so that, having

been justified by his grace, we might become heirs having the hope of eternal life. (NIV)

Imagine if we truly lived as heirs of Christ who are clothed in His righteousness. I am convinced that the enemy is on the warpath to defeat the body of Christ through our sinful choices like never before. I'm not blaming our sin on Satan, as it's our own decision to choose sin over holiness. But the enemy wants us to live in defeat to the point we believe there is no hope. The lies he roars over us may even make us wonder why we should bother turning from our destructive choices.

Thankfully, my dear Rick chose the path of righteousness—instead of destruction. He surrounded himself with a few select men who had learned, years before, to fight the good fight to walk in freedom. But more importantly, he chose to stand and live in the victory that Jesus had won for him over sin and death.

Today I can testify that Rick is the most honorable man I know, and the scars from our nearly broken marriage are now reminders of our beauty-from-ashes story. Our purpose in sharing a brief glimpse of our marriage redemption story here is so you can borrow our hope for your own story and the temptations you may be facing.

It was not easy to move forward in our marriage. As we sought wholeness and healing, the enemy tried to step up his attacks in other areas of vulnerability in our lives. That is how the enemy rolls, trying to thwart any movement toward freedom. Just like a lion attacking his prey, he looks for the weak and the injured. And that is why an understanding of how to stand strong in our victory, even at our weakest, is so critical. Rick and I can both testify that without an understanding of how to fight the enemy with God's Word and prayer, we probably wouldn't have survived the battle raging over our marriage back then.

In *The Adversary*, there are three very practical and applicable steps about walking in our victory over temptation and sin (which the Bible often refers to as "the flesh"). This is an approach that both

Rick and I try to apply to our own lives and that we have shared often with others who are seeking freedom in an area of temptation. I feel so strongly about the power of these steps that I want to share these truths exactly as they appear in *The Adversary*:

STEPS TO VICTORY OVER THE FLESH

Galatians 5 and other New Testament passages teach that we can overcome fleshly desires through three steps:

1. A walk of honesty. Be honest with yourself, recognizing some sins may be more tempting than others. The Holy Spirit wants us to be honest, to see and admit our old depraved fleshly nature. Each believer will see himself someplace in the listing of fleshly sins of Galatians 5:17–21.

Ask the Holy Spirit to show you your fleshly sins in all of their lurid ugliness. Then admit those fleshly sins that are your peculiar temptation and defeat.

2. A walk of death. When a person believes on the Lord Jesus, he or she is baptized by the Holy Spirit into the death of Jesus Christ (Romans 6:3–6). As followers of Jesus, we are united with the Lord Jesus Christ in His death, and we should consider ourselves "dead to sin but alive to God" (see Romans 6:11). Because of Christ's death and our death with Him, "we should no longer be slaves to sin—because anyone who has died has been freed from sin" (Romans 6:6–7). Victory over the flesh is always an active, aggressive, moment-by-moment appropriation of the absolute truth that "I have been crucified with Christ" (Galatians 2:20).

3. A walk in the Spirit. This resurrection life of Christ is brought into our experience as the Person of the Holy Spirit is granted fullness of control. It remains the believer's responsibility to "be filled with the Spirit" (Ephesians 5:18).

When a believer is filled with the Spirit, his or her body, soul, and spirit are controlled and directed by the enabling grace of the Holy Spirit.[3]

Also, part of walking in the Spirit is asking God to fill us every day with His fruit of the Spirit as outlined in Galatians 5:22–23, so that there is no room for that temptation to take root.

The teaching continues:

> Victory over the flesh, the world, and the devil is all provided for us. Appropriating that victory and walking in it is our responsibility. Willfully doing otherwise will lead to disaster and may require a fierce battle with Satan before freedom returns. I believe that one of the greatest needs for the church is that believers be aware of the seriousness of our battle against Satan and the practical, spiritual help that brings us victory. Such victory must be part of our daily spiritual walk.[4]

So, let's make this three-step walk practical by applying it to a possible area of temptation you might be facing. Perhaps you're being tempted to lie to your boss because of a mistake you made at work that could impact your company financially. Or, perhaps you're married but tempted to flirt with someone other than your spouse, or maybe you're hanging on to bitterness toward a friend who has wounded you.

Now let's apply the walk of honesty, walk of death, and walk in the Spirit to those situations. That could look something like this through a desperate prayer you cry out to God:

> "Dear Father God, You know how I am being tempted, and I thank You that I can run to You with this temptation to
>
> _____ . I first choose the walk of honesty. I know that I am capable of letting this temptation escalate to sin because of my sin nature. I can't fight this in my own strength. Help me to choose the walk of death over this temptation. Thank You that because of the death and resurrection of Jesus Christ, I am dead to sin and alive in Him. I'm grateful that You always provide a way to escape temptation. Help me to see it and take it. I choose to walk in the fruit of the Spirit today. I invite the Holy Spirit to fill me with His love, joy, peace, patience, kindness, goodness, faithfulness, gentleness, and (especially) self-control over this specific area of temptation or sin I am facing. Please fill me to overflowing so that there is no room for this temptation to take a foothold and destroy me. Thank You that it is Your breastplate of righteousness that covers me. I choose to stand in Your righteousness and in the victory already won for me over this temptation. May I turn the victory over this battle into an act of worship that is glorifying to You. In the name and power of the Lord Jesus Christ, I pray. Amen."

I love this declaration in Scripture that roars: "It is for freedom that Christ has set us free. Stand firm, then, and do not let yourselves be burdened again by a yoke of slavery" (Galatians 5:1 NIV).

It is for freedom that Christ has set us free! Let's choose to live in freedom instead of defeat. Jesus wants to set us free from the temptations or sins we are battling right now.

- If you are tempted today to leave your marriage for some-one else, choose Jesus.
- If you are tempted to lie, choose His truth.
- If you are tempted to slander a friend with gossip, choose the fruit of kindness and gentleness instead.
- If you are tempted to live in bitterness, choose forgiveness.

May we run to our God when temptation or sin feels as if it will consume us. Jesus already knows what we are battling and promises to provide a way of escape.

If you sense that you are being held captive or imprisoned in darkness because of an area of sin in your life, dwell in this promise: "No temptation has overtaken you that is not common to man. God is faithful, and he will not let you be tempted beyond your ability, but with the temptation he will also provide the way of escape, that you may be able to endure it" (1 Corinthians 10:13).

I remember a woman who once shared with me how she was bat-tling an area of sin in her life that kept defeating her. She was strug-gling with shame and a sense of hopelessness. I encouraged her to run to God to honestly pour out her heart to Him. But she told me that she was embarrassed or ashamed to pray, as it had been a long time since she had talked to God. She said she needed to first "clean herself up a bit" before she could approach our holy God. I knew this woman was a mom, so I asked her to imagine her little boy coming to her to confess something he'd done wrong but then turning him away—telling him to first get cleaned up or make himself present-able before she will listen to him. Of course, she said she'd never do that to her son. Then I asked her why she thought that our loving and merciful God would turn her away because of the choices she had been making.

THRONE OF GRACE

I know no better verse to cling to when feeling defeated in an area of sin in my life than Hebrews 4:16: "Let us then with confidence draw near to the throne of grace, that we may receive mercy and find grace to help in time of need."

What a beautiful picture to think of our God being the Throne of Grace. Do you believe that you will find grace if you go to God with your temptations? Do you believe you will "receive mercy and find grace" if you're honest with Him about your battle with a sin that is consuming you? Or do you think you will only find a God who is angry or disappointed with you and who wants you to clean yourself up a bit before entering into His presence?

Author and seminary professor Bill Thrasher shares a story in his book *A Journey to Victorious Praying* about a young man who was battling a destructive habit that he didn't want to give up. Thrasher encouraged the young man to go to God in all honesty about that struggle and told him he would find mercy and grace as Hebrews 4:16 promises. Thrasher writes, "To draw near with confidence means to come with freedom to the throne of grace in the authority of Christ."[5]

Later in the book, Thrasher gives some surprising but inspiring advice: "Use the temptation to do wrong as a motivation to pray. You can apply this to any persistent temptation in your own life. What if every time you are tempted to think an impure thought, you pray for the purity of your children?"[6]

Don't you love that idea? Imagine if the moment you're tempted to sin; you instead pray over a loved one who might be tempted in the same way? This could be especially powerful for aunts, uncles, parents, or grandparents who pray over the children in their lives or for future generations. (I'll cover more on this in the last chapter that focuses on the "Roar of Prayer.")

As we confront temptation, often on a daily basis, let's remember to run, not walk, to the throne of grace. Let's remember that we are covered in the breastplate of His righteousness as we battle temptation and the "sin that so easily entangles" us (Hebrews 12:1 NIV). The enemy wants us to live in defeat and hopelessness when it comes to our sin. And unfortunately, there are many followers of Christ who are giving up in defeat, thinking that their stories are not redeemable so they might as well abandon trying to live in victory over their sin. Instead, may we choose the louder roar of the authority and victory that Jesus has already won for us over sin.

We've been dwelling in Hebrews 4:16 about the throne of grace, but we also need to cling to the truth of the verse that immediately precedes that: "For we do not have a high priest who is unable to sympathize with our weaknesses, but one who in every respect has been tempted as we are, yet without sin."

I don't know about you, but it brings me great comfort knowing that truth. Jesus is our Advocate and Defender and He is the One who provides us a way of escape from every temptation.

One of the most profound films I have ever seen about the battle against temptation and sin is *The Heart of Man*. It's a beautiful movie that is sobering but also enthralling in its depiction of what God has done for us in conquering sin and death. The gorgeous cinematography pulls you in from the start as you see an old man (the God figure) and a young man (representing all of us) high upon a cliff overlooking the ocean. The God figure is playing a hauntingly beautiful song on his violin as the young man listens, even joining in the song on his own violin. But then suddenly the young man senses something (or someone) on a faraway island drawing him like a magnet to leave his first Love. He dives off the cliff, abandoning the sweet communion he had with his Father God. I don't want to give too much of the movie away as I hope you will find it online and watch it. But the God figure never stops pursuing the young man, going to hell and back to rescue him.

The scenes of the old man and young man are interspersed with true testimonials of people from all walks of life, including a man who shares his story about an addiction. He paints this beautiful picture of what it means that Christ takes on our sin for us:

> I remember I was in prison, my hands were cuffed together and I had a tray of food and I was walking in the cafeteria in prison past all these tables. And no one would let me sit with them, and I found my own table and sat down. And in walks Jesus, and He's dressed in prison clothing, like me, and He sits down across the table from me, and He doesn't say anything. And I asked Him, I said, "Will You eat another meal with me?" And, He said, "I'll eat with you anytime you want. By the way, the door is open. You can leave anytime you want." And I just . . . I melted. It's unconditional, unfailing, present love. But for Him to be with me in my addiction, and in sickness, and in relapse, over and over and over again—that's what changes me.[7]

The movie includes a scene where the young man who dove off the cliff to chase after temptation is later in a dark, cold cave—bound in chains, beaten beyond recognition. All seems lost and forsaken as he continues to be pummeled by the enemy of his soul. At first you think he's the only tortured soul in the cave, but then the camera pulls out to show many in the same condition. It is a gruesome scene, but such a picture of the grip addictive sin can have on any of us. But, more importantly, the movie is filled with a message of great hope and redemption.

HE MAKES ALL THINGS NEW

It has been almost twenty years since God began the reshaping of our marriage after Rick's brave decision to run to the throne of grace.

We've since watched our two daughters get married, Rick walking each of them down the aisle and then joining me in the front row. We've been together when meeting our newborn grandchildren for the first time on the day of their births, and we were together by my father's side when he took his last breath just shy of his 90th birthday.

I know that is not the story of all who are shattered by the choices of a loved one or by their own choices. I have friends whose spouse chose a different path, leaving their families to pick up the pieces on their own. Perhaps that is your story. I pray that you will continue to cling to the One who will never leave you, never forsake you. Remember that Jesus is the true Rider on the white horse as we see in Revelation 19:11 where His name is Faithful and True—names that I know resonate if you've been betrayed.

May you always remember the true and everlasting story the Lion of Judah is roaring over you: "Blessed assurance, Jesus is mine. Oh, what a foretaste of glory divine. Heir of salvation, purchase of God, born of His spirit, washed in His blood. This is my story, this is my song, praising my Savior all the day long."

Let's run to Him now to pour our hearts out to Him:
Jesus, help me place my temptations at Your scarred feet and to learn to walk and live in Your victory. Thank You that You see me righteous only because of Your righteousness that covers me like a breastplate. Because You were tempted as we are, You know better than anyone the battle I am facing. I know I can confidently draw near to Your throne of grace, receive mercy, and find grace from You to help me in this time of need. I'm grateful to You for not sending me away until I get my act together; instead, You embrace and enfold me with Your love and mercy. Help me stand in the victory You have already won for me. Help me choose the walk of

honesty, the walk of death, and the walk in the fruit of the Spirit when I battle temptation and sin. Thank You for being in this battle with me. In the power of Your holy name, I pray. Amen.

The Roar of His Word:

Read these verses aloud as you wield the sword of His Word against temptation and sin in your life: Galatians 5:1, 16–25; Hebrews 4:14–16; 1 Corinthians 10:13; Romans 6:5–8; Isaiah 61:1–4.

Worship Song:

"Blessed Assurance" as sung by Shane & Shane.[8]

chapter six

WHEN I
BELIEVE LIES

"If you abide in my word, you are truly my disciples,
and you will know the truth, and the truth will set you free."

JOHN 8:31–32

WHEN OUR FAMILY lived in Michigan, we had a Yorkie named Sophie. All ten pounds of her was convinced she was the size of a German Shepherd. Whenever we had deer in our backyard, she would bark ferociously until I'd let her out the door to chase them away from our flowerbeds. They'd quickly run away in fear, with Sophie yapping at their heels all the way to the end of our property. She'd then prance back in victory, pretty proud of herself for protecting her domain. She was tiny, but mighty.

Sophie's stance is such a good illustration of the type of courage we should display against our formidable foe. But she didn't always keep that bold and brave stance.

After we moved from Michigan to the mountains in Colorado, Sophie encountered a different kind of deer in our neighborhood. They are called mule deer because of their large ears. These regal creatures—often as large as five-point bucks—love to linger in the shade of our aspen trees on hot summer days. Unlike the deer in

Michigan, they are not easily spooked, and they have an air about them as if they own the place.

From our front window, Sophie would spot the mule deer and start barking at them, just like she did at the deer in Michigan. The first few times I let her outside, she'd run up to them yapping and growling; but they wouldn't budge, and gave her a look of are-you-kidding-me disdain. Sophie tried to stand her ground, but she'd soon retreat back into the house, whimpering in defeat.

We too often retreat in defeat when we let ourselves believe that the enemy is bigger, stronger, and more powerful than our Lord Jesus Christ. One of the enemy's most persistent, yet subtle, weapons (or roars) is the vicious lies he throws at us. Those lies can be like fiery darts that penetrate our armor—especially the belt of truth—when we choose to believe Satan's word over God's Word.

In John 8, we are told that Satan "was a murderer from the beginning, and does not stand in the truth, because there is no truth in him. When he lies, he speaks out of his own character, for he is a liar and the father of lies" (v. 44b).

In my years serving on staff at my church, I've noticed that one of the strongest battles followers of Christ deal with is in combatting the lies of the enemy or lies we've chosen on our own to believe as truth. We may have victory over many other areas, but the battle to keep our thoughts captive to truth is fierce, and it is one of the enemy's most vicious, yet often subtle, tactics against us.

The enemy comes at us with his murderous lies in two key areas:

1. Lies about our God (especially related to His goodness or trustworthiness)
2. Lies about ourselves (especially related to who we are in Christ, our true identity)

He's been doing this since the beginning. His weapons have always been filled with lies and deception (Genesis 3:1–7; Romans 1:25), and he will continue to try to deceive us. That is why we need to have God's truth firmly planted in our hearts and minds.

LIES ABOUT GOD

I have friends my age who have asked me to pray for their young adult children who have left their faith in Jesus—those who had once loved Him deeply, but then decided to stop loving or trusting Him because of deep disappointments in their lives or with the church. They are wrestling with questions like: *How could a loving God who allows babies to die, the horrors of cancer, or sex trafficking still be considered a loving and merciful God?*

In the past few years, there have been several followers of Christ (some well-known worship leaders, authors, and seminary professors) who suddenly announce that they've decided they are no longer a Christian. Each time their stories race across the internet, my heart sinks and I wish I could lovingly ask them, *"Does that mean you no longer believe that Jesus is real or the risen God? Or do you just not want to follow Him anymore?"*

I remember when I read *The Last Battle*, the final book in the Chronicles of Narnia series, and discovered that the older sister, Susan, was declared "no longer a friend of Narnia."[1] Her response to her siblings is telling, as their cousin Eustace explains it:

> "Whenever you've tried to get her to come and talk about Narnia or do anything about Narnia, she says, 'What wonderful memories you have! Fancy your still thinking about all those funny games we used to play when we were children.'"[2]

The first time I read that part of the story I was moved to tears. Susan had loved Aslan deeply. She had witnessed his brutal death and then his coming back to life. She had seen him defeat the witch where he brought color, warmth, and life back to Narnia. And yet, it seems as if she left her love for Aslan because of the distractions and pull of her earthly life. It's not clear if C. S. Lewis meant for his readers to think Susan would never return to her love and devotion to Aslan, but I remember it impacting me in a deep way as a warning that I can be pulled away from my deep love for Him.

The enemy's roar is often loudest when tempting followers of Jesus not to trust God's goodness and faithfulness anymore. And it seems as if that roar is getting louder. There is so much unrest in our world, where chaos and uncertainty seem to rule. Many are doubting that God is in control or questioning if He even cares. I have friends whose stories are some of the hardest I've ever heard. One was just diagnosed with cancer; at the same time, her two sisters are also battling cancer. I have other beloved friends seeking healing from their memories of childhood sexual abuse and trafficking, while others have walked through the horror of the death of a child.

Isn't that all too much to bear, Lord Jesus? Where are You in all of that? Are You still good and loving, trustworthy and kind, even in this heartache? Sorrows You could have prevented?

Perhaps you've prayed a prayer like that due to your own deep sorrows. What I love about our God is that He wants us to run to Him with those hard questions and lamenting prayers—to pour our hearts out to Him like the psalmists modeled for us so often:

> "My soul also is greatly troubled.
>   But you, O LORD—how long?" (Psalm 6:3)

> "How long, O Lord, will you look on?
> Rescue me from their destruction,
>   my precious life from the lions!" (Psalm 35:17)

"How long, O LORD? Will you hide yourself forever?"
(Psalm 89:46)

I hope you've discovered that our God can handle our hard questions and our "How long, O Lord" prayers.

But where we need to be careful is when we listen to the enemy's lying and accusing "voice" and start believing his lies about God as truth. Lies like: *Your God is cruel, capricious, and cold. He is helpless and weak. Your God is not trustworthy. He doesn't care about what you are going through. He's not even aware of it. Your God isn't even real.*

Until Jesus takes us home, we will go through many battles that are all clamoring to make us leave our first Love and doubt His goodness and mercy. When I find myself wrestling with doubts about God's goodness or sovereignty, I try to remember those who have walked through much deeper sorrows than me, and yet they still love and trust Him. I want to learn from them about how to cling to the truth that He is always good and faithful, come what may.

One of those friends is named Kim. I mentioned her briefly in the "When I Am Afraid" chapter. She lost her three-year-old son, Austin, to complications from strep throat. She actually chose to follow Christ soon after Austin's death, but she still understandably wrestled for years with trusting God's goodness and protection.

I recently asked Kim, "As a mom whose son is now in heaven, how have you learned to trust God and know that He is good, no matter what?"

This is part of her story . . .

> Coming to a place where I truly believed that God was good took a long time, actually. When Austin passed, in that moment I knew heaven was real, so I latched on to that. If that's true and real, then God has to be good. But then I had to line God's

goodness up with Scripture and all the awful things that happened in the Bible, let alone in our world. I remember crying out to Him, "You allow some really horrific things to happen on this Earth and I don't understand why!"

I soon came to realize that there is no pat answer as to why Austin died. I don't think I will ever fully understand the why of Austin's death this side of heaven, and I'm now okay with that. I don't believe it's my place to understand why or to ask God for an explanation. Coming to that place took time and solitude, crying out to Him, studying the Scriptures. I began to dwell in the New Testament and watched Jesus as He walked this Earth.

Always, He came through for His followers—not always in the way that they hoped, but He was always faithful. I saw that Jesus does what He says He will do, and that includes one day providing a new heaven and new earth and eternal life with Him in glory. That is His ultimate answer to our sorrows and questions. That is where I place my hope and trust.

In my search in the Gospels, the pivotal moment came for me when I saw Jesus on the Mount of Olives where He prayed just hours before He was arrested:

"'Father, if you are willing, remove this cup from me. Nevertheless, not my will, but yours, be done.' And there appeared to him an angel from heaven, strengthening him. And being in agony he prayed more earnestly; and his sweat became like great drops of blood falling down to the ground."[3]

Jesus was asking that the cup of death be taken from Him. There, I saw that He wept. He grieved. He was in agony. And that gave me hope. Jesus doesn't like suffering any more than we do. But I realized, like Jesus did with His Father, that I have to submit my life to Him and trust Him with it—"not my

88

will, but yours." That intimacy with Jesus comes from saying *my life is Yours*. It's that acceptance of His salvation gift where I not only said, *You are my Savior, but also my Lord, and I'll do whatever you ask. All of it belongs to You, my whole life is Yours.*

I pray that Kim's story of surrender inspires and encourages you. I know it's made a huge difference to me and I hope we remember the word of her testimony when unspeakable pain comes into our own lives.

The biggest takeaways for me from Kim's story are:

- Run to Scripture for truth to combat the lies we are believing about God.
- Ask the hard questions of God. He already knows how you feel and what you are thinking, so be real with Him.
- Then, let Him answer those questions through His Word. Study the life of Christ in the Gospels (Matthew, Mark, Luke, and John), and watch how Jesus handled pain and sorrow in His own life and the compassion He showed for others.
- Through prayer, ask God to help you surrender your whole life to Him and to trust Him with eternity in mind.

Is there a chance that you might be believing lies about God and don't even know it?

The most effective way to counter the lies or doubts we are believing about God is to search His Word for the truth of who He really is. Remember that part of our armor is the belt of truth, so let's "buckle on" securely some truths about our God. Ephesians 6:17 tells us that the Bible is the sword of the Spirit. It is the Holy Spirit–infused Word of God and it is our powerful weapon to wield against the lies that bombard our hearts and minds.

If you are a new believer, or if you're seeking more truth about Jesus, read the book of John. As you read, write down truths about Jesus' character or the attributes He demonstrated as He interacted with His disciples, healed the sick, or prayed to His Father. That is what Kim did when she found Christ soon after Austin's death and she wanted to know better the God she was trying to trust.

Or, take time to dwell in the Psalms to join the chorus of songs the psalmists wrote to proclaim truths about God's character and attributes. One of my favorite psalms that seems to shout truths about God is found in Psalm 145. If you are having doubts about God, read that psalm and write down all the truths about God you find there. Those truths can help counter the lies you have been believing about Him. Or they can help you to guard your heart against lies about Him that might come up in the future due to difficult circumstances:

> He is gracious.
> He is merciful.
> He is slow to anger.
> He is abounding in steadfast love.
> He is good to all.
> His mercy is over all that He has made.
> His kingdom is an everlasting kingdom.
> His dominion endures throughout all generations.
> He is faithful in all His words.
> He is kind in all His works.
> He upholds all who are falling.
> He raises up all who are bowed down.[4]

That list contains just some of the truths about God found in Psalm 145. Maybe you're living in those "difficult circumstances" right now, and you're having an even harder time believing those truths. Perhaps . . .

- You're struggling with believing that His "mercy is over all that he has made" due to facing cancer or losing someone to COVID.
- You've been betrayed, and you doubt that God "is faithful in all His words" or that His love is steadfast.
- You're living with infertility and don't understand how He is "kind in all His works."
- You grew up with an angry or abusive parent and can't trust that God is "slow to anger" or "upholds all who are falling."

If you are bearing any of those sorrows, cry out to God and ask Him to cement the truths of who He is in your heart and mind. He will be faithful in answering that prayer for you.

You may need to take some time as you wrestle with your questions or doubts about God. That's okay. He is ever patient with us. Ask Him to show you truths from His Word or to remind you how He has been good, merciful, or faithful to you in your past. Write those truths down in your journal so you don't forget.

And, when the enemy tries to throw lies about our God at you, pray a prayer like this (or write your own prayer to Him):

Father God, I am wrestling with believing that You are

_____ or _____ right now. I am walking through such deep sorrow, or I see such pain and chaos around me that it's hard to trust You. Thank You that I can wrestle with You and ask the hard questions. But please guard my heart and mind against the lies about You that the enemy throws at me, or that I choose to believe on my own. Thank You for the helmet of salvation that covers my mind and for Your belt of truth. I choose today to stand in the truth of who You are, no matter my circumstances or the suffering I see around me. Guard my heart and mind from doubting Your goodness and faithfulness. I praise You that one day all sorrow will be wiped away and I worship You as my compassionate, merciful, loving Savior. In Your holy name, I pray. Amen.

LIES ABOUT OURSELVES

In his book *Victory Over the Darkness: Realize the Power of Your Identity in Christ,* Neil T. Anderson writes about the devil's primary motive:

> The major strategy of Satan is to distort the character of God and the truth of who we are. He can't change God and he can't do anything to change our identity and position in Christ. If, however, the father of lies can blind our minds or deceive us into believing it isn't true, we will live as though it isn't.[5]

I'm assuming that resonates in your own life's journey as it does mine. How often have we been blinded by the enemy's lies over us or we've exchanged God's truth for lies? The battle for truth can be relentless and ruthless. I think that is probably why the apostle Paul begins his teaching on the armor by first focusing on the belt of truth. In Ephesians 6:13–14, he seems almost to shout "stand firm" to his readers and not give up. This is that battle cry: "Take up the whole armor of God, that you may be able to withstand in the evil day, and having done all, to stand firm. Stand therefore, having fastened on the belt of truth . . ."

We cannot afford to be passive in our battle for truth. We must:

Take up the whole armor of God.
  Withstand in the evil day.
    Having done all, to stand firm.
      Stand therefore.
        Fasten on the belt of truth *to stand firm.*

You've probably heard the phrase "identity in Christ" enough that it's become somewhat cliché or overused to the point the meaning can be unclear. As believers, our *true* identity is found only in Christ. It is who we are because of who He is: "If anyone is in Christ, he is a new creation. The old has passed away; behold, the new has come" (2 Corinthians 5:17). We are also called "a chosen people, a royal priesthood, a holy nation, God's special possession, that you may declare the praises of him who called you out of darkness into his wonderful light" (1 Peter 2:9 NIV).

The enemy doesn't want us to believe the truth of how God sees us, and who we are in Him because of what Jesus has done for us. The enemy is intent on snatching those truths from us through his lies to make us weak in standing against him.

In my former role as a women's ministry leader at my church, I met with women almost every week who were walking in shame because of their past choices or because of condemning words spoken over them by others. Others were letting the betrayal of a loved one define them, making them feel unworthy and unloved. God's Word tells us that the enemy is the "accuser" (Revelation 12:10) and the "father of lies" (John 8:44), and yet we so often accept those accusations and lies as truth.

COMBATTING THE LIE OF SHAME

In the book *Surprised by the Healer,* authors Linda Dillow and Juli Slattery dedicate the book to "the nine brave women who shared their stories, exalting the Healer and giving hope to countless others with broken stories." The book is filled with the stories of those nine women who walked through deep sorrow, abuse, or shame. One woman's story of abortion covered her with so much shame and condemnation that it took years for her to believe she was truly forgiven. Because Lorraine couldn't forgive herself, she believed the lie that God couldn't forgive her either. She saw this as a huge battle with the enemy:

> There is a reason so many Christian women hang on to the guilt of their sin even though they know about God's total forgiveness. There is someone who does not want you to be free; his name is Satan. He does not want God to have the glory shown through the miracle of forgiveness. He would much rather Christians walk in a cloud of shame instead of dancing in freedom and praise. Not only is Satan called the father of lies, he is also called the accuser. His job description is to make you feel guilty. Revelation 12:10 tells us that Satan accuses us before God day and night. Can you hear his voice accusing you?[6]

Lorraine goes on to share three steps we can take to combat the accusations of the enemy. You might want to get the book and study those practical steps in more detail. Briefly, they include: 1. Recognize the Voice, 2. Remember the Cross, and 3. Declare the Truth.[7] I especially appreciate what Lorraine wrote under the first step and how it relates to what we've been looking at regarding listening for *the loudest roar*:

> Recognize the Voice: When you have thoughts that bring on condemnation, can you tell the difference between God's conviction and Satan's accusations? God convicts us of sin for the sake of leading us to freedom. Our enemy taunts for the purpose of keeping us in bondage . . . God longs for you to know and receive His forgiveness for your past. Satan wants you to dwell on how bad you are. His flaming arrows (Ephesians 6:16) make you doubt that God could or would completely forgive you.[8]

I find it interesting that the next two steps: Remember the Cross and Declare the Truth were the same steps God led Kim to take as she wrestled with doubts about His goodness after Austin's death. It was because of the truth of God's Word and remembering what Christ won for us through His death on the cross that Kim was rescued from despair and turning away from the God of all hope.

THE BELT OF TRUTH

The belt of truth is the first piece of armor mentioned in Ephesians 6:14 for a reason. Truth is the core of our protective armor that holds it all together. Priscilla Shirer teaches this in her Bible study *The Armor of God,* where she does a deep dive into each piece of God's armor. She writes, "When you have a strong, stable, well-supported core, you can't easily be led astray by the enemy's clever lies. Gird yourself with truth, and you're on guard from the word 'go.'"[9]

My dear friend Becky grew up in a home filled with abuse of every kind. Her father was a pastor, often preaching on Sunday and then going home to abuse his children that same day. The fact that Becky grew up to love Jesus and His Word deeply—in spite of such horrific abuse—is truly a miracle.

As an adult, Becky realized her understanding of who God is and how He defines her was distorted due to her earthly father's abuse. In sharing her story with me recently, Becky said that for years she was afraid to think of God as her Father. Instead, she viewed Him as scary, harsh, and condemning like her earthly father. Becky shares how God used the truths in His Word to rescue her from those lies:

> I had to fight for truth about who God the Father really is. I knew and trusted Jesus the Son, but I struggled with trusting God as my Father. I asked Him to show me who He really is. I wanted to make sure I was worshiping the true God and not

some image of the God distorted because of all of my father's abuse even as the pastor of our church.

The Holy Spirit led me to Colossians 1:15 where we see that Jesus "is the image of the invisible God, the firstborn of all creation." And Hebrews 1:3 promises that Jesus "is the radiance of the glory of God and the exact imprint of his nature."

Those verses showed me that truths about God the Father and God the Son are the same. That's when I began to read through the Gospels over and over—for four straight years—to help me rediscover the true God of the Bible. I asked Him to give me a renewed understanding of who He is and how He loves me. And He was faithful in that. While reading through the Gospels, I fell in love with Jesus again and realized that that is who God the Father is: He is gracious, kind, merciful, loving, and trustworthy.

Becky also found that she had a hard time believing who God says *she* is in His Word, due to the many lies spoken over her by her father. So, again, she ran to Scripture to find the truths of how God sees her. Verses like Isaiah 43:4, where she's told "you are precious in my eyes, and honored, and I love you." And Psalm 34:4–5 gave her hope: "I sought the LORD, and he answered me and delivered me from all my fears. Those who look to him are radiant, and their faces shall never be ashamed."

I believe God rescued the lives of both Kim and Becky with the weapon of His truth through His Word countering the lies of the evil one.

What about you? What lies about yourself are roaring over you right now? I assume some come to your mind right away like they do for me.

Perhaps your list includes lies that you are not worthy enough for

God's love and forgiveness because of choices you've made that you think are unforgivable. Perhaps you've chosen to believe the lie that you have nothing to offer to serve God faithfully with the gifts and talents He's given you. The list can be long for many of us. Ask the Holy Spirit to bring any lies you've been believing about your true identity to your mind, and then write them down.

Now, as you reflect on your list, how can you counter those lies with the word of truth, God's Word?

I want to share a powerful "Who I Am in Christ" list with you. I didn't write it. The apostle Paul wrote this list while he was in a Roman prison around AD 62. I wonder if Paul—despite writing the list to believers in Ephesus—knew he too needed to cement these truths in his own heart and mind as he languished in prison. If you are a follower of Jesus, these truths from Ephesians 1 are also for you today:

- He has blessed you in Christ with every spiritual blessing in the heavenly places.
- He has chosen you to be holy and blameless before Him.
- He has predestined you for adoption to Himself as sons and daughters through Jesus Christ.
- He has blessed you with the praise of His glorious grace.
- In Him, you have redemption through His blood.
- In Him, you have the forgiveness of sins, according to the riches of His grace.
- He has lavished His grace on you, in all wisdom and insight making known to you the mystery of His will.
- In Him, you have an inheritance.
- In Him, when you heard the word of truth, the gospel of your salvation, and believed in Him, you were sealed with the promised Holy Spirit.[10]

Jesus died to give us that list. All of that "true identity" was won through His sacrificial death for us.

Nothing on that list is about anything we accomplish on our own, it's all because of Jesus. Because of Him—and only because of Him— we can know that we are blessed, chosen, predestined, redeemed, forgiven, lavished with grace, have an inheritance, and sealed with the Holy Spirit. What an amazing list, and that's just taken from thirteen verses in the Bible! Imagine if you searched God's Word to find more truths about who you are in Christ.

It's hard to believe those truths at times, isn't it? There's a loud roar that has a different list, one that looks a lot like the lies you believe about yourself. Our world shouts a different identity over us, often rooted in its standards for performance or beauty, wealth or success. We have to stand firm and counter those lies with God's truth.

Read through the list of truths above again from Ephesians 1 about who you are in Christ (out loud if it helps you focus). Linger in those truths, perhaps even pausing to thank Him for the ones that mean the most to you right now. Though those truths are unchanging, the enemy is relentless in trying to snatch them from our hearts. It's up to us to choose to actively believe and live in biblical truths instead of the lies. Ask the Lord to help you believe, and may you hear His voice above the lies, saying:

> "My sheep hear my voice, and I know them, and they follow me. I give them eternal life, and they will never perish, and no one will snatch them out of my hand. My Father, who has given them to me, is greater than all, and no one is able to snatch them out of the Father's hand. I and the Father are one." (John 10:27–30)

Pray these truths about who you are in Christ:

Lord Jesus, thank You that because of Your death and resurrection I am forgiven, redeemed, chosen, lavished with grace, and I have an eternal inheritance. Help me live in my true identity and cement those truths in my heart and mind through dwelling in Your Word. Guard my mind and heart against the lies about who I am in You. Help me keep my mind captive to truth. May Your voice of truth be the loudest over me. In Your powerful name, I pray. Amen.

Roar of the Word:

Read Psalm 145 and dwell in the truths of who God is. Then read Ephesians 1 and thank Him that that is how He sees you as His beloved child.

Worship Song:

"His Name is Jesus" sung by Phil Wickham.[11]

FINDING YOUR ROAR OF VICTORY

In the first two parts of this book, we have been looking at how Jesus is the Victor, and His unshakable victory is ours because we are His. But, I want to be careful that it doesn't seem like we don't have a strategic part to daily live in that victory. Remember the "battle cry" that we looked at in Ephesians 6:10–18? There, we saw that our armor is Jesus, that He is our protective covering. But those verses are not a passive, just-sit-back victory cry. Instead, we are told to: *Be strong. Put on. Stand against. Withstand. Stand firm. Take up. Keep alert.*

The best way to *be strong* and *stand firm* is to dwell and delight in His Word and engage in prayer daily. Those are the offensive weapons we can *take up* to help us *withstand* and *be alert*. What if instead of viewing reading and applying His Word and praying consistently as performance or duty-driven, we see His Word and the privilege of prayer as priceless gifts Jesus has given us—His "immeasurably more than we could ask for or think of" gifts for us?

In Part Three, we will learn the practical ways we can daily take up and wield the believer's mightiest weapons: the roar of God's Word and the roar of prayer.

part three

OUR
MIGHTIEST
ROARS

But we will devote ourselves to prayer
and to the ministry of the word.

ACTS 6:4

chapter seven

THE ROAR
OF HIS WORD

He who dwells in the shelter of the Most High
   will abide in the shadow of the Almighty.
I will say to the LORD, "My refuge and my fortress,
   my God, in whom I trust."

PSALM 91:1-2

PICTURING GOD'S WORD as the sword of His Spirit, as it's described in Ephesians 6:17, should embolden us to strike down every lie and temptation of the enemy. Jesus modeled this better than anyone. In Matthew 4:1–11, Jesus faced a brutal battle against Satan in the wilderness after He had been fasting for forty days. The incarnate Jesus was most likely physically and mentally exhausted when the enemy came at Him with the roars of accusations and temptations. Isn't that just like Satan, strategically attacking us when we are alone and at our weakest? Doesn't that sound a lot like a lion, patiently and stealthily stalking its prey, targeting the most vulnerable, and then charging?

But Jesus stood His ground. In this exchange between Him and the devil, it's almost as if they are engaged in hand-to-hand combat, swords drawn and clashing. Satan's sword was forged in lies and brandished with twisted words of half-truths. Jesus, even though He was physically weakened, kept picking up His sword, forged in the refining fires of the truth of God's Word, and striking His foe throughout this battle.

How stunning to see the Living Word use the written Word as His weapon of choice. Jesus didn't use long speeches or complicated arguments against Satan. When the tempter came at Him, Jesus held up the sword of the Spirit and declared "It is written." Every single time. Jesus Himself shows us that one of the most significant weapons against the enemy is God's Word.

Ironically, Satan tried using Scripture as a weapon by twisting its meaning. While tempting Jesus, he even quoted from a psalm that declares our protection: "For it is written: 'He will command his angels concerning you, and they will lift you up in their hands, so that you will not strike your foot against a stone'" (see Matthew 4:6 NIV; Psalm 91:11–12). Tragically, that is not just a strategy of the enemy as I've heard many stories from those who have been spiritually abused by others who have twisted the truth of God's Word to accuse, condemn, or shame them.

> **How stunning to see the Living Word use the written Word as His weapon of choice.**

Ultimately, this famous battle ended in victory for Jesus when He said to His enemy, "Away from me, Satan! For it is written: 'Worship the Lord your God, and serve him only.'" We're then told that "the devil left him, and behold, angels came and were ministering to him" (v. 11). I wonder how the angels took care of Jesus after such a battle. I hope we'll find out more about that when we meet Him face-to-face.

Let's choose to follow the example of Jesus and pick up our sword of the Spirit—God's Holy Word—and wield it against the same enemy who is always intent on defeating us. He has to flee when God's Word is used to defeat him. We're going to look at some practical ways to do that.

One of my favorite "battle psalms" is Psalm 91. I remember cling-ing to Psalm 91 while our family lived in China, as if it was oxygen giving me my next breath. This psalm is such a great example of how we can use Scripture as a weapon against the enemy, and against our own fears and doubts. I read and prayed Psalm 91 over my sick daughter so often during those three years that I ended up memoriz-ing it without even trying.

Years later when Kelly was an adult and married, we learned that her in-laws prayed the same psalm over our son-in-law Cal when he was a newborn with viral meningitis. What a gift to know that Kelly's future husband was being prayed over with the same promises from Psalm 91 when he was just a baby too. And now, Kelly and Cal are praying the same psalm over their own little boys.

I call Psalm 91:1 my 911 promise of rescue: "He who dwells in the shelter of the Most High will abide in the shadow of the Almighty."[1] Some consider this psalm the soldier's song because they have prayed it over their loved ones in the military when they're deployed. Others see it as a warfare psalm, teaching us how to stand strong against the enemy and abide in our victory. Though no author is mentioned in the Hebrew text of this psalm, Jewish tradition ascribes it to Moses, as he wrote Psalm 90, while others say David wrote it—a mighty war-rior himself.

Regardless of who wrote it, I know it was inspired by our Most High, Almighty God. It's a psalm filled with the wonder of the differ-ent names and attributes of God, and it declares His protection over us again and again. We are going to look closely at this psalm in this chapter, as it is a practical example of how God's Word is the sword of the Spirit (Ephesians 6:17), and how we can use it as a powerful weapon in our battles.

My father often taught on Psalm 91 as a pastor and author. When he passed away in 2017, I inherited his well-worn Bible. Of all the passages he loved the most, the pages of Psalm 91 are the most marked up with his notes. And the margins are yellowed from his strong hands that held his Bible open to that page throughout the decades, most likely as he prayed those truths over our family. He also viewed Psalm 91 as a warfare psalm that proclaims the promises of our protection and victory in Christ.

Read the whole psalm out loud—as a victory roar over you and your own family. Memorize it if you can. Rick and I memorized Psalm 91 together when we were praying for our marriage or when we'd pray for our daughters.

Notice in just the first two verses, we see several majestic names and attributes of God: He is the Most High. He is Almighty, He is LORD. He is our shelter. Our refuge. Our fortress. All of those names and attributes communicate to us the power of His protective covering over us.

But we have a part in that sheltering, protective place. Do you see how we are not to take a passive role? Instead, we need to dwell, to abide, and to trust in Him. When the storms of doubt or fear or sin threaten to consume you, remember that we can *choose* to dwell in the shelter of our Most High and rest in the shadow of the Almighty.

I've already touched on some ways to do this through memorizing key Scriptures, praying God's Word, and dwelling on the lyrics of worship music that minister to your heart and mind while facing temptation or trials. May we never forget that our Most High, Almighty God is our refuge and fortress, and it is in Him that we can trust!

Don't you love that picture of being able to abide or rest in His shadow? Typically, for someone to cast a shadow on us, we have to be very near to them. What a powerful picture of the guarding presence of our God. And yet, how often we leave that protective shadow due to the choices we make.

Psalm 91 goes on to describe God's protection over us:

Surely he will save you
from the fowler's snare
and from the deadly pestilence.
He will cover you with his feathers,
and under his wings you will find refuge;
his faithfulness will be your shield and rampart. (vv. 3–4 NIV)

Save. Cover. Refuge. Faithful Shield. Rampart.

During the start of the COVID-19 pandemic, I noticed those verses were often quoted in sermons, text messages, or in online memes and blogs. We can all more readily relate now to the fear of "deadly pestilence." Unfortunately, I also saw posts that were not accurate, claiming these verses promise complete protection from dangerous viruses if believers have enough faith. But that is not truth, and that is not what this passage promises. I don't believe these verses are talking about earthly pestilence and diseases, but about the "fowler's snare" in the spiritual realm as described in Ephesians 6:12 (NIV):

For our struggle is not against flesh and blood,
but against the rulers, against the authorities,
against the powers of this dark world and
against the spiritual forces of evil in the heavenly realms.

We have been dwelling a lot in Ephesians 6, which outlines God's armor of protection that covers us. Thankfully, in spite of the battle Paul describes in Ephesians, Psalm 91:4–5 promises us that God will save us from the snare and deadly pestilence of our enemy, the fowler. Psalm 91 is even so bold to proclaim in verses 9–10 (NIV) that:

If you say, "The LORD is my refuge,"
and you make the Most High your dwelling,
no harm will overtake you,
no disaster will come near your tent.

Those are tricky verses for people who have endured sorrows like the death of a loved one, childhood sexual abuse, domestic violence, or the ravages of natural disasters, such as the forest fires and hurricanes that have destroyed many "tents" in the last few years. You may be asking if those promises are for you today due to the tragedies that have come near or ravaged your own life. Perhaps your raw question when reading those verses is: "Really, God, no disaster will come near my tent? That hasn't been the case in my life."

I am not saying that these verses promise that no harm will ever befall us, as some have wrongly interpreted these verses. I do know that God promises never to leave or forsake us in the storms that threaten to overtake us. That doesn't mean we won't be hit with deep suffering and sorrow; it means that God's faithfulness is our shield and rampart in whatever storms we are in. Remember my mom and her sticky note that read, "I'm fading away, but Jesus is keeping me every day"? Outwardly, she was wasting away, and God chose not to heal her. But inwardly she knew God was keeping her soul safe, and His comfort and peace sustained her until she saw Him face-to-face.

Like Jesus, may we hide His Word in our hearts to be ready when the battles come. Try memorizing Psalm 91 as your victory cry, and pray it often over your life and for your loved ones. If you're a young mom, pray it when fear grips your heart for your little ones. Or perhaps you are longing for a message of hope as you go through uncertainty about your health or the heartache of betrayal. Run to His Word and stand in the truth that your Most High, Almighty God is your shelter, refuge, and fortress.

Recently, God used this same psalm to comfort my questioning heart about my father's suffering from cancer. He had served his God faithfully for almost ninety years and yet still suffered at the end of his life. Soon after his death, I was dwelling in Psalm 91 early one morning and wrestling with the whys of his death. As I read the last two verses, it was as if the Holy Spirit was saying, "Judy, even with your father's suffering, I was *with him in trouble, I rescued him and honored him, and with long life I satisfied him and showed him my salvation*" (Psalm 91:15–16).

Do you see what God did there? Two decades after He calmed my fearful heart for my toddler in China, He used the same promises to comfort my grieving heart for my elderly father.

OUR EYES ARE ON YOU

There's a story in Scripture that is a powerful picture of how God fights our battles for us and with us. The story is found in 2 Chronicles 20 and reads like scenes from an epic film. Though it's about a king who lived long ago, the choices he made when facing the threat of an ominous battle can be a blueprint for us today in our own battles.

In the few chapters leading up to the dramatic story, we meet a king named Jehoshaphat, who is ruler over the kingdom of Judah around 849 BC. We are told he was a godly king, bringing his people "back to the LORD, the God of their fathers" (2 Chronicles 19:4). By chapter 20, King Jehoshaphat is warned that "a great multitude is coming against [him] . . . from beyond the sea" (v. 2). There were actually several armies who were intent on joining forces to destroy the king and his people. It would have been an unwinnable battle . . . except for God.

Upon learning of this threat, Scripture tells us of the king's response:

> Jehoshaphat was afraid and set his face to seek the LORD, and proclaimed a fast throughout all Judah. And Judah assembled to seek help from the LORD; from all the cities of Judah they came to seek the LORD.

And Jehoshaphat stood in the assembly of Judah and Jerusalem, in the house of the LORD, before the new court, and
said, "O LORD, God of our fathers, are you not God in heaven?
You rule over all the kingdoms of the nations. In your hand
are power and might, so that none is able to withstand you."
(2 Chronicles 20:3–6)

You can read all of the king's prayer in verses 3–12; and then he
ends his prayer with these words that probably resonate with how
we often feel about the battles we are facing: "For we are powerless
against this great horde that is coming against us. We do not know
what to do, but our eyes are on you" (v. 12).

What a heartfelt and humble prayer from a king who was afraid:
"We do not know what to do, but our eyes are on you." Have you
prayed a prayer like that before? I wish I had more often, rather than
trying to fight my battles in my own strength and not keeping my
eyes on Him.

As we study this story in Scripture, we can see how the king's
prayers and actions show us this pattern to follow when we encounter
our own fierce battles:

- He first set his face to seek God (v. 3).
- He proclaimed a fast (v. 3).
- He assembled with others to seek the Lord (v. 4).
- He turned to prayer (v. 5).
  - started with worship (v. 6)
  - remembered God's faithfulness in the past (vv. 7–8)
  - stood firm in the pending battle (v. 9a)
  - cried out his requests and trusted to be heard (vv. 9b–12)
- He listened to wise counsel (vv. 13–17).

Right after his prayer is finished, we see that "all of Judah stood before the LORD, with their little ones, their wives, and their children" (v. 13). Don't you love that? All of Judah—even the little ones—heard the prayer of their humble (and scared) king. And right there in their midst, someone delivers a divine message that probably sounded too good to be true. He tells them:

> "'Do not be afraid and do not be dismayed at this great horde, for the battle is not yours but God's. . . . You will not need to fight in this battle. Stand firm, hold your position, and see the salvation of the LORD on your behalf, O Judah and Jerusalem.' Do not be afraid and do not be dismayed. Tomorrow go out against them, and the LORD will be with you." (2 Chronicles 20:15, 17)

Stand firm. Hold your position. And see the salvation of the LORD on your behalf. These verses offer a powerful example we can follow for our own roar of victory! Come back to this story when you need it the most. You can pick up God's Word—the sword of the Spirit—and hold up these same truths from these verses against the wars you face with fear, temptation, lies, and doubts:

- Do not be afraid.
- Do not be dismayed.
- The battle is not yours but God's.
- Stand firm.
- Hold your position.
- See the salvation of the Lord on your behalf.
- The Lord will be with you.

Immediately after that battle cry, God's Word tells us: "Then Jehoshaphat bowed his head with his face to the ground, and all Judah and the inhabitants of Jerusalem fell down before the LORD, worshiping the LORD" (v. 18).

That's a scene I so wish we could see in real time. Just imagine the king and *all* the inhabitants of Judah and Jerusalem falling down before God and worshiping Him before they faced their enemies. And that surrendered worship happened even before God won the battle for them the next day!

The next morning when they headed out to face their adversaries, King Jehoshaphat first appointed worshipers who "were to sing to the LORD and praise him in holy attire, as they went before the army, and say, 'Give thanks to the LORD, for his steadfast love endures forever'" (v. 21).

What a story! The king set up an army of worshipers to lead his army into battle, all the while giving thanks to God and proclaiming the truth that His love is steadfast, enduring forever. We're told that when they began to sing and praise, the LORD set an ambush against the other armies coming for them. Armies from at least three different areas fought each other before ever reaching the king and his people—and those armies ended up killing each other (v. 24).

They never even had to enter into the battle with earthly swords or weapons. Instead, they became an army of worshipers and prayer warriors who trusted God to deliver them. Oh, that we may dwell in this story from God's Word and march forth in surrendered worship and prayer . . . no matter our circumstances or the cost of that surrender to trust. Let's cling to God's Word. Savor it. Hide it in our heart and mind. Wield it against the enemy's lies. Run to God's Word when we are tempted to run away from God. Pray it over our children and grandchildren, spouses, and aging parents. Pray it when we question His goodness and mercy when battling chronic illness, infertility, temptation, or defeat.

If you dwell in His Word, God will use His promises—and epic true stories written thousands of years ago—to bring hope and comfort, and life and victory to your frightened or grieving heart today.

Join me in this prayer based on the opening verses of Psalm 91:

"Loving heavenly Father, I make my choice to dwell, to abide in the provided protection, the safe shelter of Elyon, Your shelter! As the highest of the high, I affirm that You have provided me all that I need to keep me safe in the person and work of my Lord Jesus Christ. My Lord Jesus Christ is Your shelter for me. Because You are El Shaddai, the Almighty, omnipotent One, I rest in the shadow, the watchful close presence of Your person and power, despite the noise and schemes of the darkness around me. I affirm my LORD, my personal, loving Father: You are my refuge, my safe place and my fortress, my fortified protection, my God, my Elohim, in whom I trust, the One who includes the Father, the Son, and the Holy Spirit.

With confidence I affirm that You will save me from the fowler's snare. Satan is the cruel fowler who uses his subtlest craftiness to try to take me captive, to rob me of my freedom, and to destroy me. He keeps coming at me in his deadly, pestilent ways to unsettle and confuse my assurance of my safety in You. I look to You to cover me with Your feathers like a mother hen covers her little chicks under her watchful eyes and powerful wings. Thank You that the Lord Jesus Christ stayed on the cross until His work there for me was complete. He gave His life in death to provide me forgiveness and Your safety from judgment and the snare of the fowler. It is Your faithfulness that shields me and provides a rampart of protection that hides me in the fierce battles addressed against me by darkness and evil."[2]

The Roar of His Word:

Read Psalm 91 out loud to cement those truths in your heart and mind today. Better yet, try to commit to memorizing the first four verses.

Worship Song:

"Psalm 91 (On Eagle's Wings)" as sung by Shane & Shane.[3]

chapter eight

THE ROAR
OF PRAYER

And pray in the Spirit on all occasions
with all kinds of prayers and requests.
With this in mind, be alert and
always keep on praying for all the Lord's people.

THE APOSTLE PAUL, EPHESIANS 6:18 (NIV)

WHEN I WAS LEADING a very busy ministry, I happened upon a quote that stopped me in my too-busy-to-pray ministry tracks:

> I have often thought about what my greatest surprise will be when I go home to be with the Lord. After much pondering, I have concluded that it will be the tremendous power and peace that was available to me through prayer on this side of heaven—and how infrequently I used it![1]

Ouch! Talk about convicting. And I'd guess that "infrequent use" also resonates with your own prayer journey, either now or in the past.

In *The Screwtape Letters* by C. S. Lewis, the protagonist, a demon named Screwtape, writes this in a letter to his nephew and minion, Wormwood:

Once you have made the world an end, and faith a means, you have almost won your man, and it makes very little difference what kind of worldly end he is pursuing. Provided that meetings, pamphlets, policies, movements, causes, and crusades, matter more to him than prayers and sacraments and charity, he is ours—and the more "religious" (on those terms) the more securely ours.[2]

Prayer is often elusive for us, isn't it? I know I have been there. May we not let that continue to be our story, where the enemy wins by keeping us from prayer because we are so busy serving God or because we are apathetic or bored with prayer. What if, instead, we could discover a fresh commitment to being prayer warriors together? Through this chapter, we will learn to move from talking about the importance of prayer to actually praying in confidence, boldness, and the Holy Spirit's power.

The enemy wants to keep us from prayer because he is threatened when God's people pray. That's why I think Paul's teaching about the armor ends with focusing on the importance and power of prayer. I used to think his teaching on the armor ended with verse 17 about the sword of the Spirit, God's Word. But notice how Paul ends his armor-focused teaching on the power of prayer in verse 18 of Ephesians 6 (NIV): "And pray in the Spirit on *all* occasions with *all* kinds of prayers and requests. With this in mind, be alert and *always* keep on praying for *all* the Lord's people."

Wow! Do you see the preeminence of prayer in that verse—the "allness" of it? It's easy to view prayer as an "add on" or bonus to our walk with Christ and not to see prayer as a key to intimacy with Him and how we can dwell in the shelter of Him.

Remember when earlier we looked at how we are seated with Christ now and that He is interceding for us to the Father? What a remarkable and sacred gift that we can talk to the One who is high and lifted up, seated on the throne, but also whose Spirit dwells within us. How astonishing we've been given full access to the triune God in prayer.

I actually see prayer as one, if not, *the* most important part of the armor for us. And, I think that is why the enemy tries to distract us from prayer.

I want to end this book with some practical ways to awaken a revival of prayer so that we truly "*always* keep on praying" until He calls us home. Does your prayer life need a revival or fresh start? Do you want to discover new ways to be a consistent prayer warrior? Then please read on, and you'll find ideas for igniting the mighty roar of prayer in your own life and ministry.

LEAVING A LEGACY OF PRAYER

My grandmother, Nessa Bubeck, was the quintessential prayer warrior you often hear about and hope to be. She raised five boys on an Iowa farm during the years of the Great Depression and World War II. Grandma also had a baby girl she named Lilah Mae who only lived three days, while all of Lilah's brothers went on to live into their eighties and nineties.

Like all of us, my grandmother's life wasn't perfect. She struggled with depression, most likely due to her deep grief over losing Lilah Mae. But I think it was because of those dark times in her life that her love for Jesus grew deep, and she became a mighty and consistent prayer warrior.

Much of Nessa's life was marked by prayers over her sons and their families. She told us that when they were younger, she often whispered short prayers, like, "Oh, God, keep them" when she'd see her teenage boys racing down the country roads on tractors or horses. Other times she prayed through the night, worried about her toddler who was battling pneumonia, and years later she'd pray for that same son who was questioning his faith as a teen. That son was my own dad, who grew up to carry on her legacy as a prayer warrior over his own family.

One of my favorite memories of my grandmother was when I had her—and the whole farm—all to myself one glorious week in the summer of my thirteenth year. I was the youngest of three girls and was born right in the middle of my grandmother's sixteen grandchildren. So, I was thrilled that I didn't have to share Grandma with my siblings or cousins that week.

I loved waking up to the sound of the old windmill outside my window, and I'd often run out to pump a glass of water from the windmill into the old tin cup that hung on a rusty hook nearby. I'd help feed the hens and gather their eggs for breakfast, or I'd watch my grandfather plowing the fields or feeding the hogs. Then, in the afternoons, Grandma would teach me to crochet or bake yummy cakes from scratch. And she even let me drive her car down the farm's gravel road, three years shy of my sixteenth birthday.

Just eighteen months after that grand week in Iowa, my grandparents weren't with us anymore. One cold December morning as they were headed to town on a country road, their car hit a patch of black ice and went careening down a steep embankment. They were both killed instantly. I was only fourteen.

A few days after their funeral, the postman dropped off our mail through the slit in the front door. I saw a light pink envelope with my grandmother's beautiful handwriting among the other envelopes. It was addressed to me and dated December 3, 1974, just a week before the car accident that took them to glory.

I'm looking at that letter now as I write this, almost fifty years after it was mailed to me:

Dearest Judy: Was so good to talk to you last evening. My it is beautiful here this A.M. Trees are all covered with 2 inches of frost. I said to Grandpa, wish I could take a picture of that . . .

She then goes on to mention she's praying for my older sister who was pregnant with my grandmother's first great-grandchild:

I am so happy about the baby coming, and I will be happy to be great grandma and you will be auntie. Am sorry Rhonda is not so good, I can really sympathize with her. I was always so sick too. Tell her I shall be praying for her. I must write to her.

Nessa then ended her letter with:

I want to go see all of you this winter if possible . . . Jesus loves us all doesn't He, I don't think I realize His great love as I should. Tell Mother and Daddy we love them. Grandma

My grandmother never got to visit us that winter or meet her first great-grandchild, born six months after the accident. But the legacy of her life continues to ripple through all of our lives to this day. The greatest gift my grandmother gave us was her decades of prayers over her five sons and their children and future generations. That was her legacy. Oh, how I long to one day be remembered as a prayer warrior like Nessa Bubeck.

Perhaps you're thinking, *I wish I'd had a praying grandmother or father, but I didn't have a praying anyone!* But how amazing if you choose to become the first person in your family who leaves a legacy of prayer. I have many dear friends, all more dedicated to prayer than I, who have had the joy and privilege to be the first in their family to pick up the baton of prayer for their future generations.

THE WONDER OF PRAYER

A few years ago at a conference for ministry leaders, the keynote speaker said that when he first chose to follow Christ, the wonder of knowing Him took his breath away. But then he got so busy in ministry he felt like he was just out of breath serving God. He had lost the wonder.

As he spoke, I knew that was also my story. On my drive home, I cried out to God, asking Him to restore wonder to my walk with Him, to take my breath away because of the beauty of His Word and what He has done for me. And I asked Him to deepen my heart for prayer. I wanted to have a sense of awe and wonder that we have the privilege of prayer and that God wants us to come to Him in prayer.

As we look at the "wonder of prayer," you'll learn practical and creative ways to awaken and deepen your passion for prayer. May these truths grow you into a mighty warrior of prayer. All these ways begin with the letter "w" to help you remember these ideas and apply them to your own prayer life. A core verse is included for each prompt.

Worship Prayers

"I will extol you, my God and King, and bless your name forever and ever. Every day I will bless you and praise your name forever and ever." *(Psalm 145:1–2)*

Years ago, God brought a beloved mentor into my life. Joanie was known as a prayer warrior, and she asked if she could be my prayer partner where we'd commit to getting together about once a week to pray. Joanie was the one who taught me to begin our time of prayer together in worship, rather than jumping right into praying over requests to God.

Like a skilled music teacher, Joanie began to teach me the song of worship when we prayed together. Often, we'd begin our prayer time together by playing worship music to prepare our hearts. I now often do that on my own in the morning before I pray. It is astonishing how the music quiets my mind from all the distractions and turns my heart toward God in worship.

Joanie also taught me to begin our time in prayer by worshiping God, which helped us focus our minds on Him, more than on ourselves. Sometimes we'd use the Alphabet Praise to begin our prayers, going through the alphabet by worshiping Him through His names and attributes. For example:

> We worship You as our **A**lmighty God.
> You are the **B**read of Life.
> You are **C**ompassionate.
> You are my **D**eliverer and my **E**verlasting **F**ather.
> You are **G**ood.
> You are **H**oly, Holy, Holy.
> You are our **I**nfinite and **J**ust God.
> I worship You as our **K**ing of kings and **L**ord of lords!
> You are **M**ajestic, yet **N**ear to the brokenhearted.
> You are **O**mnipotent and **P**owerful.
> You **Q**uiet our hearts.
> Thank You, Jesus for being my **R**edeemer and **S**avior.
> You are **T**rustworthy and **U**nderstanding.
> You are **V**ictorious and **W**orthy of all my praise!

The letter "x" gets little tricky, but you get the idea. And I love to end that alphabet praise by declaring He is **Y**ahweh and **Z**ealous for us!

I began to use that alphabet worship even with our daughters as we drove in the car, where we'd take turns coming up with His different names as we prayed together. The next time you pray, try to begin your time in worship and praise of our God. Listen to a worship song or sing one of your own as a way of expressing the wonder and celebration of being able to enter into His presence in prayer.

Word of God Prayers

"If your law had not been my delight, I would have perished in my affliction. I will never forget your precepts, for by them you have given me life." (Psalm 119:92–93)

In the most painful seasons of my life, I have clung to His Word as if it was giving me my next breath. God's Word truly became my delight and there were times that I believe "I would have perished in my affliction" if I hadn't run to the truth of His Word. Praying God's Word back to Him can also be one of the most effective ways to quiet the roar of the enemy over our lives. I call that Word of God prayers.

Reading Scripture out loud is a great way to begin your prayer time in worship and praise. I love to read psalms of praise like Psalms 145–147, Psalm 95:1–7, or Psalm 100. Those are just a few examples of how to turn to praise and thanksgiving through praying His Word, even in the storms of this life. I find it inspiring that David wrote many of the psalms while he was running for his life from his enemies. Often, David was hiding in caves while he wrote his songs of praise and worship.

Praying Scripture over loved ones is a powerful way to intercede and calm our fears for them. For example, I prayed Psalm 139 over my babies when I was pregnant with them. Years later, I prayed Psalm 91 over our daughters when I was gripped with fear for their safety and health. Then, as they grew older, I'd turn prayers written in Scripture into prayers on their behalf, like Colossians 1:9–14, outlined below. I've come to realize that one of the main ways to "dwell in the shelter of the Most High and rest in the shadow of the Almighty" (Psalm 91:1) is through praying God's Word.

One of my favorite prayers to now pray for our five grandchildren (who are all babies and toddlers as I write this book) is found in Colossians 1:9–14. It's a prayer Paul wrote for the people in Colossae. How awesome that we can take Paul's prayer and make it our own today. Here are the highlights of that prayer and how to pray it for others:

Father God, may I (or my loved ones) . . .

- be filled with the knowledge of Your will
- be filled with spiritual wisdom and understanding
- walk in a manner worthy of You
- be fully pleasing to You
- bear fruit in every good work
- increase in the knowledge of You
- be strengthened with all power according to Your might
- endure with patience and joy
- give thanks to You, our Father, who has qualified us to share in Your inheritance

That powerful prayer starts in the New International Version with, "since the day we heard about you, we have not stopped praying for you." Oh, that that would be true as I strive to be a prayer warrior over my grandchildren throughout the rest of my life.

Do you see how you can pray God's Word to calm your fears, to turn to praise and worship, and to pray scriptural truths over loved ones? Those are just a few ways to use God's Word in prayer. We've already looked at how God's Word—the sword of the Spirit—is our offensive weapon against the enemy, and I hope these ideas will help you as you use that sword against the enemy in prayer.

Weeping or Wrestling Prayers

"How long, Lord? Will you forget me forever? How long will you hide your face from me? How long must I wrestle with my thoughts and day after day have sorrow in my heart? How long will my enemy triumph over me?" (Psalm 13:1–2 NIV)

I love those heart-wrenching questions that the psalmist David cried out to God in Psalm 13. His words seem to give us permission to cry out with our own weeping or wrestling prayers.

Have you ever prayed your own "How long, Lord" prayers?

How long, Lord, will I battle depression?

How long, Lord, do I have to wait for a baby?

How long, Lord, will I pray before my prodigal comes back to You?

How long, Lord, until I find answers for this chronic illness?

How long, Lord, until I walk in freedom?

How long will You hide Your face from me?

How long must I wrestle with my thoughts and day after day have sorrow in my heart?

How long? How long? How long, Lord?

Singer and blogger Jane Kristen Marczewski—who went by the stage name Nightbirde—passed away from cancer at just thirty years old in early 2022. Just months before, she had captured the attention of millions by singing a song she wrote while competing on the television show *America's Got Talent*. Soon after winning the opportunity to advance immediately to the live shows, she dropped out of the competition due to her illness. It wasn't until after her death that I read this post she had written on her blog, which is such a powerful example of what it means to wrestle with God while still trusting Him:

I am still reeling, drenched in sorrow. I am still begging, bargaining, demanding, disappearing. And I guess that means I have all the more reason to say thank you, because God is drawing near to me.

Again.

Again.

Again.

No matter how many times He is sent away.[3]

I believe that weeping and wrestling prayers can be part of our worship as we cry out to God. It took me a long time to learn this and a season of sorrow upon sorrow before I realized that lamenting prayers can draw us closer to Him. God wants us to come to Him with our sorrows and questions. Jesus showed us this in His own lamenting prayers when He walked this earth, so why do we often pull back from going to God with prayers that are real and raw, full of our despair and questions?

In the foreword to the book *A Sacred Sorrow: Reaching Out to God in the Lost Language of Lament* by Michael Card, Eugene Peterson writes:

It's an odd thing. Jesus wept. Job wept. David wept. Jeremiah wept. They did it openly. Their weeping became a matter of public record. Their weeping, sanctioned by inclusion in our Holy Scriptures, a continuing and reliable witness that weeping has an honored place in the life of faith. . . . Why are Christians, of all people, embarrassed by tears, uneasy in the presence of sorrow, unpracticed in the language of lament? It certainly is not a biblical heritage, for virtually all our ancestors in the faith were thoroughly "acquainted with grief." And our Savior was, as everyone knows, "a Man of Sorrows."[4]

I can testify that some of my sweetest times in prayer have been when I've run to God with my wrestling or weeping prayers. During a particularly trying season in my life, I would often linger in the Psalms. I found hope and comfort in the psalms of lament, especially those written by David.

I also began to notice that while David spent a lot of time lamenting in prayer, he often then turned to praise after pouring out his sorrows and questions. I started to follow David's rhythm of lament and praise, and found that brought life and hope to my weary soul.

Card also talks about lament and praise in *A Sacred Sorrow:*

> Depending on which commentary you pick up, you'll read that from one-third to over one-half of the psalms are laments. With the exception of one psalm (88), each lament turns eventually into praise, revealing an important truth that has been lost; lament is one of the most direct paths to the true praise we know we have lost.[5]

Try this in your own prayer journey. Get a journal where you can pour out your "How long, Lord" prayers to Him. You can even write out lamenting psalms as your own prayer over whatever situation you are currently enduring. Then, try turning to praise, even in your sorrow.

Following David's rhythm of lament and praise has brought life and hope to my weary soul.

During the healing time in our marriage story, I sensed that God was asking me to turn to praise even in the midst of my deep sorrow. The Psalms often refer to this as a "sacrifice of thanksgiving" (see Psalms 50:14, 23; 107:22; 116:17). At first, I didn't understand why He was asking me to thank Him, and I was somewhat incredulous, as if it was presumptuous of God to expect praise from me when I was suffering.

But out of obedience, I began to scribble down some of the things I could be thankful for.

First, I'd pour out my sorrows in my prayer journal, and then at the end of the prayer, I'd list things I was thankful for, even in the midst of those sorrows. Or, I'd write out a list of ways He had rescued me in the past to remind myself that He is and will always be faithful to the end. Those sacrifices of thanksgiving became my worship.

Psalm 77 is a great example of pouring out our hearts to Him and then turning to praise. The psalmist begins with a long list of laments or questions (vv. 1–9), but then reaches back to remember God's faithfulness in the past (vv. 10–12):

> *Then I said, "I will appeal to this,*
> *to the years of the right hand of the Most High."*
> *I will remember the deeds of the LORD;*
> *yes, I will remember your wonders of old.*
> *I will ponder all your work,*
> *and meditate on your mighty deeds.*

I pray that you can find your own list of "I will remember your wonders of old" while still praying your "How long, Lord" lamenting prayers. When the enemy tries to take you under with sorrow, turn to prayers of praise. When you question God's goodness today, choose prayers of remembrance and meditate on His mighty deeds in the past.

Written Prayers

"Trust in him at all times, O people; pour out your heart before him; God is a refuge for us." (Psalm 62:8)

I find when I am in a battle that writing out my prayers helps keep my mind focused and captive to truth. Writing your own prayers can be one of the best ways that you can pour out your heart before

Him if you tend to get distracted in prayer. I love to look back at the prayers of lament and praise I wrote in my journal during the fiercest storms of my life as a reminder of His faithfulness, kindness, and goodness even when it seemed like darkness was hiding His face.

Remember you can also choose a psalm or other passage of Scripture and write it as a prayer for others. I have a friend who is doing this for her grandchildren, and she hopes to give them her prayer journals for them when they are older.

Writing out your prayers is a key way to maintain your focus in prayer and keep your mind from wandering to your to-do list or other distractions. This isn't the only way to pray, but try writing out your prayers on occasion, and see how God might use that to draw you into deeper communion with Him. Below you'll find some creative ways to start a "Wonder of Prayer" journal.

WONDER OF PRAYER JOURNAL

If you'd like to try journaling your prayers, consider getting a new journal or notebook and write "Wonder of Prayer" on the cover. Write prayers during significant times in your life: a birth of a new child or grandchild, a new job; during a season of lamenting or questioning or a season when you know you need to praise and thank Him more. You could also create different sections using the categories taught in this chapter: Worship Prayers, Alphabet Praise (or Names of God) Prayers, Word of God Prayers, Weeping and Wrestling Prayers, I Will Remember His Faithfulness Prayers, or whatever categories you want to use.

Besides prayers that we write out, there is also great value in reading and praying prayers that have been written by others. One of the most common requests I get when I teach on prayer at retreats or conferences is for copies of the prayers written by my father or other prayer warriors. So, at the end of this book, you'll find "The Sound of the Roar of Prayer," which includes the Psalm 91 prayer my father wrote and prayers I've written based on the armor in Ephesians 6 and the song of worship in Psalm 139.

My husband and I love to pray written prayers aloud together, alternating paragraphs, as we pray God's Word over us or for our loved ones. (You can also visit my website at judydunagan.com where you'll find more written prayers.)

One of my favorite books of written prayers is *The Valley of Vision*, a compilation of Puritan prayers written long ago by those who have gone before us. You'll find one of those prayers at the end of this chapter that focuses on our victory and the armor of God.

PRAYER WARRIORS

You are now well-equipped to raise a mighty roar of prayer through the Word, Worship, Wrestling or Weeping, and Written prayers by others or ones that you journal on your own. These prayers are all part of the mighty roar of Warfare Praying.

Earlier, I shared the story of Joanie to encourage you to seek out a prayer partner who will commit to praying with you and for you. Joanie helped keep me accountable to pray, and God used our prayer times together to ignite a new passion for prayer in my life and ministry. Joanie was also the one who was there for us when we sensed the enemy coming at our family over the years.

As Joanie warred for us in prayer, she told me about a story she read of two friends who were biking in the hills of California when suddenly one of the women was attacked by a mountain lion. The animal knocked her down and gripped her head in his jaws. Her friend began to scream for help, but she also hung onto the woman's legs so the lion couldn't drag her away.[6] Those screams for help brought other bikers to their rescue, and the lion fled. I'll never forget when Joanie told me that's how she saw her persistence to pray for our family. She'd say, "I'm hanging on to your legs in prayer, and the roaring lion cannot devour you!"

Praying in community can be so life-giving, even life-saving. Start with asking God to connect you with someone who will pray for you and who you can pray for too. He may guide you to a friend or family member. You can also join a small group at church to pray with regularly and discover together how God can start a prayer revival among you.

TRULY LIVING IN HIS UNSHAKABLE VICTORY

Through this book, you've been given the tools to consistently pick up your mightiest weapons of God's Word and prayer, and to dwell (and rest) in the protective covering of His armor each day. But more importantly, I pray that you have found Jesus in these pages. May we never forget that His roar is the loudest and that He hems us in from all sides—guarding, protecting, and covering us. Remember that He is our safe refuge, mighty fortress, and strong deliverer. That doesn't mean that we won't grow weary in facing battles until the day He calls us home or returns for us. But may we rest in the truth that there will be a day when all those battles will cease and we will reign with Him in victory forever.

Just hours before His crucifixion, Jesus spoke these words of hope over His disciples that are just as true for us today:

"I have said these things to you, that in me you may have peace. In the world you will have tribulation. But take heart; I have overcome the world" (John 16:33).

He is our peace. He is our victory. Take heart!

The Roar of His Word:
Join in this song of praise in heaven—Revelation 5:9–14.

Worship Song:
"Hymn of Heaven" sung by Phil Wickham.[7] To hear all of the songs recommended in the book, visit judydunagan.com to access the "Loudest Roar Worship" playlist.

Read the prayer on the next page out loud as your own roar of victory.

The Servant in Battle — A Puritan Prayer

O Lord,
I bless thee that the issue of the battle
between thyself and Satan
has never been uncertain,
and will end in victory.
Calvary broke the dragon's head,
and I contend with a vanquished foe,
who with all his subtlety and strength
has already been overcome.
When I feel the serpent at my heel
may I remember him whose heel was bruised,
but who, when bruised, broke the devil's head.

My soul with inward joy extols
the mighty conqueror.

Heal me of any wounds received
in the great conflict;
if I have gathered defilement,
if my faith has suffered damage,
if my hope is less than bright,
if my love is not fervent,
if some creature-comfort occupies my heart,
if my soul sinks under pressure of the fight.
O thou whose every promise is balm,
every touch life,
draw near to thy weary warrior,
refresh me, that I may rise again
to wage the strife,
and never tire until my enemy is trodden down.

The Roar of Prayer

Give me such fellowship with thee
that I may defy Satan,
unbelief, the flesh, the world,
with delight that comes not from a creature,
and which a creature cannot mar.
Give me a draught of the eternal fountain
that lieth in thy immutable, everlasting love
and decree.
Then shall my hand never weaken,
my feet never stumble,
my sword never rest,
my shield never rust,
my helmet never shatter,
my breastplate never fall,
as my strength rests in the power
of thy might.[8]

THE SOUND
OF THE ROAR
OF PRAYER

THIS "SOUND OF THE ROAR OF PRAYER" was created to give you some written prayers, drenched in Scripture, that you can pray out loud or use as a guide to write your own Scripture-based prayers. The first one is a prayer dwelling in Psalm 91 written by my father, Mark Bubeck. The second is a prayer I wrote that focuses on the armor in Ephesians 6, and the last one is a prayer based on Psalm 139 to pray when you are fearful or burdened for a loved one.

Use the following prayers to pray over yourself, your family, your ministry, and our world. You can also use them as examples of how to pray Scripture back to God in worship or as intercession for others. When you pray God's Word, you are picking up the mighty weapon of the sword of the Spirit and wielding it against the enemy. Sometimes when a battle seems especially intense, or if you are in a place where you are finding it hard to pray, written prayers—based in the truths of God's Word—can provide you with the words to pray.

My husband Rick and I often pray together using the Psalm 91 prayer included here. We'll each read a part of the prayer aloud, alternating paragraphs. We've had sweet seasons of praying that way together, especially when we have a prayer burden for a loved one or we sense the enemy stepping up his attacks.

May God use these prayers to awaken a new heart for prayer in all of us.

1. Psalm 91 Warfare Prayer
2. Armor of God Prayer
3. Praying Scripture for Loved Ones

Find more prayers at judydunagan.com.

PSALM 91 WARFARE PRAYER
BY MARK I. BUBECK[1]

Loving heavenly Father,

I make my choice to dwell, to abide in the provided protection, the safe shelter of Elyon, Your shelter! As the highest of all the high, I affirm that You have provided me all that I need to keep me safe in the person and work of my Lord Jesus Christ. He is Your shelter for me.

Because You are El Shaddai, the Almighty, omnipotent One, I rest in the shadow, the watchful close presence of Your person and power, despite the noise and schemes of the darkness about me. I affirm of my Lord, my personal, loving Father, "You are my refuge, my safe place and my fortress, my fortified protection, my God, my Elohim, in whom I trust, the One who includes the Father, the Son, and the Holy Spirit."

With confidence I affirm that You will save me from the fowler's snare. Satan is the cruel "fowler" who uses his subtlest craftiness to try to take me captive, to rob me of my freedom and to destroy me. He keeps coming at me in his deadly, pestilent ways to unsettle and confuse my assurance of my safety in You. I look to You to cover me with Your feathers like a mother hen covers her little chicks under her watchful eyes and powerful wings. Thank You that the Lord Jesus Christ stayed on the cross until His work there for me was completed. He gave His life in death to provide me forgiveness and Your safety from judgment and the snare of the fowler. It is Your faithfulness that shields me and provides a rampart of protection that hides me in the fierce battles addressed against me by darkness and evil.

The kingdom of darkness comes at me in so many varied ways of fearsome intent. In Your provision, I choose to not fear the terrors the prince of darkness tries to put on me in the night. I choose to wear the shield of faith that quenches all of his blazing missiles that fly at me every day. I choose to not fear his wicked spirits and, sometimes, wicked people under his control who stalk me in their darkness, looking for any opportunity to strike at me. I know that the fowler tries to use his plagues of evil to destroy me, even at midday. Thank You that Your safe shelter keeps me safe from fearing such persistent, evil intent.

Thousands of the fowler's victims are falling by my side. There are tens of thousands of wounded, bleeding, hurting ones who have fallen all around me, but You promise that this destruction will not come near those of us dwelling in Your shelter. I know that Your safety is provided for believers, not to make us feel proud and superior to those who are victims. Your purpose is that we may get down where the wounded, hurting victims lie, bind up their wounds, pour in Your healing oil of the Gospel, and help set the captives free. Loving Lord, I ask You to help me see the deadly punishment that wicked acts and attitudes bring into human lives. Grant to me wisdom and Your compassion to love and care deeply for them.

With the psalmist, I choose to make the "Most High" my dwelling, my abiding place. I affirm again the Lord to be my refuge, my Person of safe protection. I look to You that none of the fowler's intended harm will befall me or any member of my family. I ask that none of his intended disasters for any within Your tent of protection will be able to touch us with their evil purposes. Thank You for Your promise of commanding Your holy angels to assist believers and protect us in this battle with the evil one and his powers. Thank You that they guard me and show me their tender care by lifting me in their hands when evil intentions want to make me stumble and fall. I praise You that You have indeed put the evil one under my feet. I choose in Your love and grace to tread upon the devouring intentions of the lion and the cobra. Help me to trample that counterfeit lion who roars his opposition to my doing Your will. Keep the attacking poison of the serpent trampled in crushing defeat under my feet.

I do love You, Lord, and declare that love in prayer. I look forward to that time You have planned in our redemption when our love will not have any of the soil of our sins hindering its expression. Thank You, for Your promise to rescue those who love You. In the security and meaning of Your lofty names, I seek Your protection. Help me to increase my prayer times of calling upon You and experiencing Your answers of mercy and grace. I look to You to be with me and help me walk in victory in my times of trouble. You are the only One who can deliver me from the evil intent of the kingdom of darkness. Thank You that You promise to honor me with Your honor. That is the only honor that really counts and it lasts for eternity. You are the One who gives me life and health in the satisfying measure that You know I need. Thank You that when this life is over in Your appointed time, You will allow me the joy of seeing my Salvation, the Lord Jesus Christ, in all of His Glory and power.

In His name, I place this prayer before You, heavenly Father. Amen.

ARMOR OF GOD PRAYER
BY JUDY DUNAGAN

Dear Victorious King Jesus,

Today I join the mighty chorus of worship, proclaiming "Worthy is the Lamb who was slain, to receive power and wealth and wisdom and might and honor and glory and blessing! . . . To him who sits on the throne and to the Lamb be blessing and honor and glory and might forever and ever!"[2]

You are worthy of all of my honor and praise this day. Thank You for covering me in Your protective armor from the top of my head to the tip of my toes.[3] May I remember that You hem me in from all sides and that You are my shelter and my strong deliverer.

Your Word promises that I can live in the strength of Your mighty power today. I choose to dwell in the unshakable victory You have already won for me. I am grateful that I can wear Your whole armor confidently and securely because I am Yours.

I choose to fasten on the belt of Your truth to guard me against the lies and the schemes of the enemy. Your Word tells us that the enemy is the father of lies,[4] and I know I am prone to believing those lies. May the roar of Your truth over me silence the roar of the enemy's lies. May Your voice through Your Word be the loudest over me, and may I keep my thoughts captive to Your truth. In the name of the Lord

2. Revelation 5:12–13b.
3. See Ephesians 6:10–18.
4. See John 8:44.

Jesus Christ, I reject the lies that the enemy and my own temptations throw at me today. And, I choose to stand and live in Your truth.

I put on Your breastplate of righteousness. Thank You that I am righteous because of Your righteousness that covers me like a breastplate. You have promised when I am tempted You will provide a way of escape for me.[5] Help me choose that escape and to live in Your victory over sin this day. Your Word tells me that "the weapons of our warfare are not of the flesh but have divine power to destroy strongholds."[6] In Your strength, I can destroy those strongholds of sin that have held me captive for too long. [Pause and see if the Lord brings to mind anything to confess to Him today.]

I choose to walk in the peace that only You can provide. I know that because You are near I don't have to be anxious about anything. Your Word promises me a peace that goes beyond my human understanding, especially if I come to You in prayer. May Your peace guard my heart and my mind as I trust in You no matter what circumstances I encounter today.[7] And may I always be ready to share the peace of Your gospel with a hurting world.

Jesus, I choose to hold tightly to my faith in You as my shield that can "extinguish all the flaming darts of the evil one."[8] I am so grateful that Your faithfulness is my shield.[9] When the enemy tries to defeat me, may I keep my eyes on You as my defender, my protector, my mighty shield.

---

5. See 1 Corinthians 10:13.
6. 2 Corinthians 10:4.
7. See Philippians 4:6–7.
8. Ephesians 6:16.
9. See Psalm 91:4 NIV.

Thank You for the helmet of Your salvation that covers and guards my mind. May I fill my mind with the truth of Your Word. I want to follow Your example, Lord Jesus, where each time the enemy comes at me with lies and temptations, I hold up the sword of the Spirit—Your Word—against him.[10] Teach me to love and treasure Your Word, to hide it in my heart, to savor it, and to never take it for granted.

I pray that You will also deepen my heart for prayer. Oh, what a privilege it is to enter into Your throne room through prayer. I want to worship You and honor You through the mighty roar of prayer each day. Thank You that You intercede for me at the right hand of the throne of God. And may I intercede for others that You bring to my mind.

In the name and power of my Lord Jesus Christ, I choose to pick up these weapons of my warfare and stand today in the victory You have won for me through Your death, resurrection, and ascension. Amen.

---

10. See Luke 4:1–13.

PRAYING SCRIPTURE FOR LOVED ONES
BY JUDY DUNAGAN

When I was expecting our first baby, Christie, I memorized Psalm 139 and began to pray it over her months before I held her in my arms. Anticipating that we were moving to Brazil right after her birth, I often wrestled with anxiety about that move with a baby. God used His Word to calm my anxious heart. Years later, I have prayed this same psalm for all of my grandchildren before they were born and for our daughters as they carried them. May this be a helpful example of how to pray Scripture to turn your fear for others into prayers on their behalf. (You can also insert the name of your loved one as you pray.)

Father God,

Thank You for the beautiful words of Psalm 139 that were written thousands of years ago by David. Thank You that I can use this song of worship as a prayer over my loved ones today.

> *You are the one who created my child's inmost being.*
> *You knit her together in her mother's womb.*
> *I praise you because she is fearfully and wonderfully made;*
> *your works are wonderful,*
> *I know that full well.*

Help me trust that You love my child even more than I do. You are her Creator and sustainer. Help me remember that . . .

> *Her frame was not hidden from you*
> *when she was made in the secret place,*
> *when she was woven together in the depths of the earth.*

Your eyes saw her unformed body;
    all the days ordained for her were written in your book
    before one of them came to be.

You know my fears and concerns for my child. Thank You that this same psalm promises that You hem her in from behind and before, and that You lay Your hand upon her. May I abide and trust in that protective covering over her today.

How precious to me are your thoughts, God, for my loved one!
    How vast is the sum of them!
Were I to count them,
    they would outnumber the grains of sand—
    when I awake, I am still with you.[11]

Thank You for being so close to my heart in prayer. Thank You that Your Word teaches that You intercede for us at the right hand of the throne of God. May I pray through the watches of the night with You over my loved one. Thank You for turning my fears into prayers for her. I love You. I worship You. I trust You. In the name of Jesus, I pray. Amen.

---

11. Prayer adapted from Psalm 139:5, 13–18 NIV.

GOING DEEPER

(QUESTIONS FOR SMALL GROUPS OR BIBLE STUDIES)

THIS GOING DEEPER BONUS is a practical way for you to go deeper with the content of the book—either on your own or in a small group, book club, or Bible study setting. You will also be able to dwell more in some of the Scriptures mentioned. And you'll find questions and journaling prompts to help you apply the truths taught in the book to your own life.

INTRODUCTION AND CHAPTER 1: COURAGE, DEAR HEART

1. What area in your life do you need someone to speak "Courage, Dear Heart" over you?

2. How does the truth that God is the bigger Lion with the louder roar over the enemy give you courage for the battle you are facing?

3. Read 1 Peter 5:7–11. How does the quote from Mark Bubeck's book, "Satan roars to make us afraid and thus more vulnerable, but our purchased right is courage to resist him" bring hope to you?

4. How has Jesus proven to be your Mighty Fortress or Strong Deliverer in your life in the past? Does that give you courage for what you are facing right now?

5. Write a prayer pouring out your heart to God about the area where you need courage the most.

CHAPTER 2: THE REIGNING KING

1. What did you find most interesting, or encouraging, about the truth that Jesus is seated at the right hand of God the Father as our reigning and ascended King?

2. Read Hebrews 12:1–2. How do those verses give you hope in your own story?

3. What are some ways that you have learned to "fix your eyes on Jesus" when the storms of life threaten to overtake you?

4. What does it mean to you that the Holy Spirit groans in prayer and that Jesus is interceding for you right now at the right hand of God? (Romans 8:26, 34)

5. Have you ever had a season in your life where it was hard to pray because the pain was too deep? If you feel comfortable, share about that now with your group, or journal about it on your own.

6. If you are in a groaning season of life, try writing out your own prayer of lament/sorrow to God. Or write a prayer about the fears you are facing.

CHAPTER 3: GOD WITH US

1. Read Isaiah 57:15. How are you encouraged by the truth that our God (who is high and lifted up) is also our Immanuel (the God who dwells with us)?

2. Remembering how Christie's coworkers surrounded her in protection in Africa, how have you experienced God's guarding and protective cover over you?

3. Read Stephen's story in Acts 7 and pay attention to how you see Immanuel in that story. (Stephen's story shows us Jesus doesn't always rescue us from hard circumstances, but He is always *with us* in them.)

4. What area in your life do you need to truly know He is your Immanuel, that He is with you just like He was with Stephen in his darkest hour? (Share this with your group if you feel comfortable.)

5. Knowing it is one of the enemy's most strategic tactics to defeat us, have you ever questioned your faith in Christ because of deep sorrow or pain in your life? If yes, what rescued you from turning away from your faith?

CHAPTER 4: WHEN I AM AFRAID

1. Do you battle anxiety or fear? If yes, in what areas? If not anxiety, what other area of your life do you think you're the most vulnerable for the enemy to come at you?

2. Read Psalm 46. Underline all the promises in that psalm of how God protects us. For example, in verse 1, underline *refuge, strength, very present help in trouble.* Which of those promises mean the most to you right now?

3. Read Psalm 139:5–10. How have you seen that Jesus hems you in from all sides in your own life?

4. Which pieces of the armor in Ephesians 6:10–18 mean the most to you in your present circumstances and why?

5. Have you had your own fiery furnace or lion's den situation in your life where it was evident that Jesus was in the fire with you, even if He didn't change those hard circumstances? If so, write about that here.

6. If you are still waiting for His rescue, can you write an "even if He does not" prayer of surrender to Him like the young men thrown in the furnace in Daniel 3?

CHAPTER 5: WHEN I AM TEMPTED

1. Have you had your own "this wasn't supposed to be my story!" situation in your own life? If so, write about that here. (Share with your small group if you're comfortable doing that.)

2. How did God meet you or comfort you in that pain?

3. Write the definition of "righteous" below. How does it encourage you that the breastplate of God's righteousness covers you even with the temptations you might be facing?

4. Review the walk of honesty, walk of death, and walk in the Spirit as outlined in chapter 5. How can you apply those steps in your own life today in an area where you are being tempted? Pray the written prayer provided after those steps and insert the name of the temptation you are struggling with as you pray that prayer.

5. Read 1 Corinthians 10:13 and Galatians 5:1. How do those verses bring hope to you? Write one of those verses below to help you remember those truths.

6. Are you struggling in your marriage? If so, what part of Judy and Rick's marriage story encouraged you for your own marriage story?

CHAPTER 6: WHEN I BELIEVE LIES

1. As you reflect on lies you have believed about God—either in your past or even now—try writing out a list of those lies here or in your journal:

Lies I have believed about God:

_____   _____

_____   _____

_____   _____

_____   _____

_____   _____

2. Now turn to Psalm 145:8–19. Read those verses aloud as a song of praise to Him. Then, either circle all of His attributes or gifts to us in those verses in your Bible, or write them here as a list you can go back to when you are doubting His goodness or faithfulness to you. (Hint: you can also find the list in chapter 6.)

Truths about God from Scripture:

_____   _____

_____   _____

_____   _____

_____   _____

_____   _____

3. Which of those truths are you finding hard to believe about God and why?

4. Ask God to reveal those truths about Him through His Word, and write those references here.

5. Now, let's look at the lies you have believed about yourself—either in your past or even now—and try writing out a list of those lies here or in your journal:

Lies I have believed about myself:

_____	_____
_____	_____
_____	_____
_____	_____
_____	_____

6. Let's counter those lies with truth from God's Word. In chapter 6, we looked at the list from Ephesians 1 about truths of who we are in Christ. Now it's your turn to create your own "True Identity in Christ" list. What truths do you know about who you are because of what Jesus has done for you? You can search the Bible for your list. Ask God to show you how He sees you. He will be faithful in that. Besides Ephesians 1, you can also find more truth about who you are in Christ in Ephesians 2, Psalm 103, and Psalm 139.

My "True Identity in Christ" List:

_____ _____

_____ _____

_____ _____

_____ _____

_____ _____

CHAPTER 7: THE ROAR OF HIS WORD

1. Turn to Psalm 91, read the first four verses, and write them below. Try memorizing those verses soon.

2. In your Bible, circle all the names and attributes of God in Psalm 91:1–2. In the English Standard Version those include: shelter, Most High, shadow, Almighty, LORD, refuge, fortress, and God.

3. Which of those names and attributes mean the most to you right now and why?

4. Now go back and underline your part in that sheltering place: dwell, abide, say (proclaim), trust. Ask God to help you to learn to truly dwell, abide, and trust in Him, and list some ways to start doing that now.

5. Which of those actions are hardest for you to do right now and why?

6. How has God used His Word to rescue you in your past?

7. Write a prayer for yourself or a loved one, based on Psalm 91:1–4.

CHAPTER 8: THE ROAR OF PRAYER

1. How would you describe your own prayer life at this time? Is it hard for you to pray or hard to find the time to pray? Write out your thoughts here:

2. What has helped you in the past to find time to make prayer a priority? If you're meeting in a small group, share creative ways you've found to revive a heart for prayer.

3. After reading about the different aspects of the "Wonder of Prayer," which of the ideas (Worship, Word of God, Weeping or Wrestling, Written Prayers) mean the most for your own prayer journey and why?

4. Try one of these ideas for prayer this week and then share with your group what idea you appreciated the most and why:

   Worship Prayer—Play worship music or begin your time in prayer by using the Alphabet Praise to worship God through His names and attributes.

   Word of God Prayers—Open your time in prayer by reading a psalm out loud, or pray a portion of Scripture for a loved one you want to pray for this week.

   Weeping or Wrestling Prayer—If you are currently carrying a deep burden, pour your heart out to God through a weeping or wrestling prayer.

   Written Prayers—Pray one of the written prayers included in this book, or write out your own prayer.

5. Consider finding a prayer partner or small group you can consistently pray with. Write down a first step you will take to do that.

ACKNOWLEDGMENTS

To my husband, Rick, and our daughters and sons-in-law: Christie and Brandon, Kelly and Cal, and our darling grandchildren. You are all proof that "every good and perfect gift is from above, coming down from the Father of the heavenly lights" (James 1:17 NIV). You are my dearest treasures this side of heaven.

To my acquisitions editor, Trillia Newbell, and developmental editor, Amanda Cleary Eastep. You have both become dear friends who not only provided your editing expertise, but also covered me in prayer as I wrote this book.

To the hardest working staff I've ever known, my colleagues at Moody Publishers, including marketers Melissa Zaldivar and Ashley Torres, and publicist Janis Todd. You all do everything with excellence for His glory and fame.

To my many friends who prayed, coached, and cheered me on as I wrote this book, including Erica, Heather, Linda, Joanie, Becky, Erin, Jenn, Kelly, Kim, Crickett, Anita, and to my sisters, Rhonda and Donna. I love you all and am forever grateful for each one of you.

NOTES

INTRODUCTION

1. See 1 Peter 5:8.
2. See Genesis 3:1; Job 1:6–12; Zechariah 3:1–2; Matthew 4:1–11; John 8:44; 2 Corinthians 4:4; 1 Peter 5:8; Revelation 2; 12; and 20:1–3.

CHAPTER 1

1. "5 Lion Wild Facts," Wild in Africa, July 25, 2020, https://wildinafrica.store/blogs/blog/5-lion-wild-facts.
2. C. S. Lewis, *The Voyage of the Dawn Treader* (New York: HarperCollins, 1952), 201.
3. Mark I. Bubeck, *Warfare Praying: Biblical Strategies for Overcoming the Adversary* (Chicago: Moody Publishers, 2016), 16.
4. See Deuteronomy 18:9–12; Acts 19:18–19.
5. I will be teaching more on the armor in Part Two of this book. I've also included a prayer I've written based on the armor as outlined in Ephesians 6 in the "Sound of the Roar of Prayer" section in the back of this book.
6. Martin Luther, "A Mighty Fortress" (1529), trans. Frederick H. Hedge (1852), as printed in the *Psalter Hymnal* (Gray), 1987, https://hymnary.org/text/a_mighty_fortress_is_our_god_a_bulwark.
7. Keith & Kristyn Getty, "A Mighty Fortress," track 10 on *Sing! Global: Live at the Getty Music Worship Conference*, Getty Music Label, LLC, 2021. Original lyrics written by Martin Luther, 1529.

CHAPTER 2

1. Some of these truths were shared in an online devotional written by Judy Dunagan titled "Faithful to the Finish Line, Day 8: Seated in Power," Revive Our Hearts, https://www.reviveourhearts.com/articles/faithful-finish-line-day-8-seated-power.

2. Darrell L. Bock, *Luke Volume 2: 9:51–24:53* (Grand Rapids: Baker Academic, 1996), 1945.

3. Hope A. Blanton and Christine B. Gordon, *Luke: Part 3, A Study of Luke 17–24* (Omaha, NE: 19 Baskets, 2020), 107.

4. "1270 Right Hand of God," Dictionary of Bible Themes, Bible Gateway, https://www.biblegateway.com/resources/dictionary-of-bible-themes/1270-right-hand-God.

5. Watchman Nee, *Sit, Walk, Stand* (Carol Stream, IL: Tyndale, 1977), 8.

6. See Revelation 20:10.

7. Dane Ortlund, *Gentle and Lowly: The Heart of Christ for Sinners and Sufferers* (Wheaton, IL: Crossway, 2020), 77. Used by permission.

8. Ibid., 78–79.

9. Heather Holleman, *Seated with Christ: Living Freely in a Culture of Comparison* (Chicago: Moody Publishers, 2015), 27.

10. Andrew Peterson, "Is He Worthy?," track 8 on *Resurrection Letters (Vol. 1)*, Centricity Music, 2018.

CHAPTER 3

1. Shane & Shane, "He Will Hold Me Fast," track 7 on *Hymns, Vol. 1*, Wellhouse Records, 2018. Original lyrics written by Ada Habershon, 1906.

PART TWO AND CHAPTER 4

1. *The Valley of Vision: A Collection of Puritan Prayers & Devotions*, ed. Arthur Bennett (Edinburgh, Scotland: The Banner of Truth Trust, 1975), 328–29, banneroftruth.org. Used by permission. Find the entire prayer at the end of the book.

2. Charles Dickens, *A Tale of Two Cities*, abr. ed. (New York: Puffin Books, 2009), 3.

3. Steve Green, "When I Am Afraid," track 5 on *Hide 'Em In Your Heart: Bible Memory Melodies (Vol. 1)*, Keepers Branch Recs, 1990.

4. Kathryn Post, Religion News Service, November 16, 2021, https://religion news.com/2021/11/16/the-chosen-christmas-special-hits-theaters-breaks-records.

5. David Jeremiah, "Daniel: Overcoming the Lion's Den," Overcomer Arena Series, Huntsville, Alabama, https://www.davidjeremiah.org/television.

6. Kim Erickson, *Surviving Sorrow* (Chicago: Moody Publishers, 2020).

7. Danita Jenae, *When Mountains Crumble* (Chicago: Moody Publishers, 2022).

8. Priscilla Shirer, *The Armor of God* (Nashville: LifeWay, 2015), 65.

9. Mark I. Bubeck, *Warfare Praying: Biblical Strategies for Overcoming the Adversary* (Chicago: Moody Publishers, 2016), 98.

10. Christy Nockels, "Head to Toe: The Armor of God Song," track 4 on *Be Held: Lullabies for the Beloved*, Keepers Branch Recs, 2017.

11. MercyMe, "Even If," track 5 on *Lifer*, Fair Trade Services, 2017.

12. Lauren Daigle, "Rescue," track 5 on *Look Up Child*, Centricity Music, 2018.

CHAPTER 5

1. "Blessed Assurance," words by Fanny J. Crosby, music by Phoebe P. Knapp, 1873. Public domain. Though she was blinded as an infant due to a botched medical procedure and years later lost her only child in infancy, Fanny Crosby chose a life of eternal significance, writing the lyrics to over 8,000 hymns.

2. *Merriam-Webster*, s.v. "righteous (adj.)," accessed March 23, 2022, https://www.merriam-webster.com/dictionary/righteous.

3. Mark I. Bubeck, *The Adversary: The Christian Versus Demonic Activity* (Chicago: Moody Publishers, 2013), 40.

4. Mark I. Bubeck, *Warfare Praying: Biblical Strategies for Overcoming the Adversary* (Chicago: Moody Publishers, 2016), 21.

5. Bill Thrasher, *A Journey to Victorious Praying: Finding Discipline and Delight in Your Prayer Life* (Chicago: Moody Publishers, 2003), 34.

6. Ibid., 42.

7. *The Heart of Man*, directed by Eric Esau (2017), Los Angeles: Sypher Studios, DVD.

8. Shane & Shane, "Blessed Assurance," track 9 on *The Worship Initiative, Vol. 19*, 2020, the Worship Initiative. Lyrics by Fanny J. Crosby (public domain).

CHAPTER 6

1. C. S. Lewis, *The Last Battle* (New York: HarperCollins, 1984), 169.

2. Ibid.

3. Luke 22:42–44.

4. Adapted from Psalm 145:8–14.

5. Neil T. Anderson, *Victory Over the Darkness: Realize the Power of Your Identity in Christ* (Bloomington, MN: Bethany House, 2020), 46.

6. Linda Dillow and Dr. Juli Slattery, *Surprised by the Healer: Embracing Hope for Your Broken Story* (Chicago: Moody Publishers, 2016), 70.

7. Ibid., 71–72.

8. Ibid., 71.

9. Priscilla Shirer, *The Armor of God* (Nashville: LifeWay, 2015), 44.

10. Based on Ephesians 1.

11. Phil Wickham, "His Name is Jesus," track 7 on *Hymn of Heaven*, Fair Trade Services, 2021.

CHAPTER 7

1. This section on Psalm 91:1 was adapted from the author's blog post, "Psalm 911," judydunagan.com, April 17, 2021, https://judydunagan.com/2021/04/17/psalm-91-1.

2. A portion of a prayer written by Mark I. Bubeck and based on Psalm 91:1–4, copyright 2004, all rights reserved. Find the entire prayer in "The Sound of the Roar of Prayer" at the end of this book.

3. Shane & Shane, "Psalm 91 (On Eagle's Wings)", track 7 on *Psalms, Vol. 2*, 2015, The Worship Initiative. Based on Michael Joncas's composition, 1979.

CHAPTER 8

1. Richard A. Burr, *Developing Your Secret Closet of Prayer* (Chicago: Moody Publishers, 1998), 8.

2. C. S. Lewis, *The Screwtape Letters* (New York: HarperCollins, 1942), 34–35.

3. Jane Kristen Marczewski, "Bald Girl in the Dark," October 30, 2020, https://www.nightbirde.co/blog/2020/10/30/bald-girl-in-the-dark.

4. Michael Card, *A Sacred Sorrow: Reaching Out to God in the Lost Language of Lament* (Colorado Springs: NavPress, 2005), 11.

5. Ibid., 21.

6. Kimi Yoshino, David Haldane, and Daniel Yi, "Lion Attacks O.C. Biker; Man Found Dead Nearby," *Los Angeles Times*, Jan. 9, 2004, https://www.latimes.com/archives/la-xpm-2004-jan-09-me-lion9-story.html.

7. Phil Wickham, "Hymn of Heaven," track 2 on *Hymn of Heaven*, Fair Trade Services, 2021.

8. "The Servant in Battle—A Puritan Prayer," *The Valley of Vision: A Collection of Puritan Prayers & Devotions*, ed. Arthur Bennett (Edinburgh: The Banner of Truth Trust, 1975), 328–29, banneroftruth.org. Used by permission. Poetry lines centered.

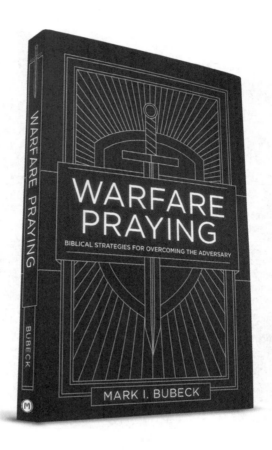

WHY IS IT SO HARD TO PRAY?

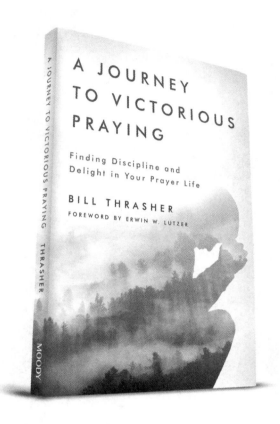

It's something many Christians can relate to: the desire to pray but the failure to execute. *A Journey to Victorious Praying* will tell you why this is and how to move past it. Pastor and author Bill Thrasher addresses common misconceptions about prayer and offers biblical truths and practices to help you gain momentum in your prayer life.

978-0-8024-1563-9 | also available as an eBook